# CONSTRUCTION
## VEHICLES TO CROCHET

Publisher: Paul McGahren
Editorial Director: Kerri Grzybicki
Design: Lindsay Hess
Layout: Jodie Delohery
Project Illustrations: Megan Kreiner
Stitch & Technique Illustrations: Carolyn Mosher
Photography: Danielle Atkins
Technical Editor: Tian Connaughton

Cedar Lane Press
PO Box 5424
Lancaster, PA 17606-5424

Paperback ISBN: 978-1-950934-57-7
e-Pub ISBN: 978-1-950934-58-4

Library of Congress Control Number: 2021934041


10 9 8 7 6 5 4 3 2 1

Note: The following list contains names used in *Construction Vehicles to Crochet* that may be registered with the United States Copyright Office: Berroco; Berroco Comfort; Bosal In-R-Form; ByAnnie Soft and Stable; Clover Amour; Craft Yarn Council; DreamWorks; Facebook; Fairfield; Fiskars; Hobbs Bonded Fibers; MKCrochet; NuFoam.

To learn more about Cedar Lane Press books, or to find a retailer near you, email info@cedarlanepress.com or visit us at www.cedarlanepress.com.

# CONSTRUCTION
# VEHICLES TO CROCHET

Chunky Trucks and Marvelous Machines Straight from the Building Site

Megan Kreiner

CEDAR LANE PRESS

# CONTENTS

**FLATBED TRUCK**

**DUMP TRUCK**

**CEMENT MIXER**

**FRONT LOADER**

**BACKHOE**

**STEAMROLLER**

## CRANE

## EXCAVATOR

## BULLDOZER

## FORKLIFT

## SKIDSTEER

## BUILDING MATERIALS

# INTRODUCTION

My kids love everything about construction vehicles. The dirt, the noise, the size of the machines, and the massive scope of construction projects ensures that if there's a work site nearby, we'll need to make a stop to check it out.

In this book, you'll find a wide selection of super-chunky construction vehicles that are sure to be a big hit with the little foremen and forewomen in your life! With pivoting joints, spinning drums, and tipping dumpers, these vehicles are loaded with all kinds of great details to make any young heavy machinery expert very happy!

Happy Crocheting!

*Megan Kreiner*

# TOOLS AND MATERIALS

Because the projects in this book are going to be well-played with, it's always worth using the best-quality materials to keep your hard work from wearing out too quickly!

## YARN

All the projects in this book were made using Berroco's Comfort Chunky bulky-weight yarn. You can find the colors used listed on the material sources page (page 117) in the back of this book and can purchase them online or through your local yarn shop. You can also use your favorite bulky-weight yarn or lighter weight yarns (such as worsted or fingering) to make smaller vehicles, but be sure to adjust your hook size accordingly to ensure a tight stitch.

## STUFFING

In addition to polyester fiberfill, which is readily available at most craft stores and will maintain its loft over time, I also recommend picking up the following materials to help maintain some of the more unique shaping found in the patterns in this book:

- **1-inch (25mm)-thick cushion foam:** Washable polyester-based upholstery foam that is available in sheets or rolls
- **Foam stabilizer:** Sew-in foam stabilizer in white and black (I used Bosal In-R-Form and ByAnnie)
- **Plastic craft canvas:** Available in white or black

## CROCHET HOOKS

Crochet hooks come in a variety of materials, sizes, and handle styles. It's ideal if you can hold and try out a hook or two out before purchasing. All of the projects in this book were made on a Clover Amour hook, size I (5.5mm). My personal preference is for a hook with an ergonomic handle to keep my fingers from cramping up.

For the most accurate sizing, refer to the millimeter measurements when selecting a hook for your project. You can also refer to the chart on page 114 for crochet hook sizes.

When making toys, it's important to make your stitches as tight as possible so the stuffing inside won't show. If you find that your stitches aren't tight enough, reduce your hook size to reduce the gaps.

## NEEDLES

A few large/jumbo steel tapestry needles are a must for when it's time to assemble your vehicles. Skip the plastic needles as they tend to bend. In addition to purchasing good strong needles, also consider picking up a small needle case for easy storage.

## SCISSORS

When working with yarn and various cuttable stuffings like cushion foam and foam stabilizer, a good pair of fabric or sewing scissors will make for clean cuts and quick snips.

## NOTIONS AND STORAGE

Here are a few more goodies to add to your crochet toolbox!

- **Stitch counter:** A row or stitch counter will help you keep track of where you are in your pattern.
- **Marking pins:** These are super-helpful in positioning your pattern pieces before sewing everything together.
- **Split or locking rings:** Use these plastic rings to help keep track of the end of your rounds or for when patterns call out for "place markers" (pm) to mark useful landmarks on your work.
- **Automatic pencil and sticky notes:** Great for jotting down notes and sticking them into your book as you work.
- **Permanent marker:** A marker is helpful to mark your foams prior to cutting.
- **Project bags:** A small project bag (like a pencil or makeup case) is great for storing smaller tools and notions; a larger bag can hold everything you need for your current project. I find that reusable canvas shopping bags make great project bags!

# CROCHET STITCHES

Whether you are brand new to crocheting or are a seasoned pro, this section will provide a complete overview of all the stitches used for the patterns in this book as well as some great tips and tricks on how to get the best results out of your work.

## Slipknot

1 Make a loop with a 6-inch (15cm) tail. Overlap the loop on top of the working yarn coming out of the skein.

2 Insert your hook into the loop and under the working yarn. Gently pull to tighten the yarn around the hook.

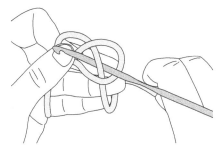

## Yarn Over (YO)

Wrap the yarn over your hook from back to front.

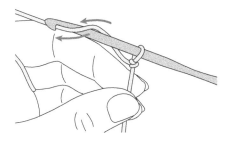

## Chain (ch)

1 Make a slipknot on your hook.
2 Yarn over and draw the yarn through the loop on your hook. You will now have 1 loop on your hook with the slipknot below it.

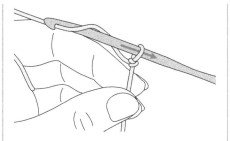

3 Repeat step 2 until you've made the number of chain stitches specified in the pattern. When checking your chain count, remember that only the chains below the loop on the hook should be counted.

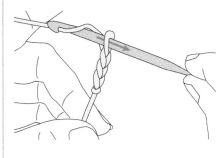

## Slip Stitch (sl st)

Insert your hook into the next chain or stitch. Keep your tension as loose as possible, yarn over, and draw the yarn through the stitch and the loop on your hook.

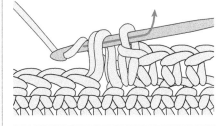

## Single Crochet (sc)

1 Insert your hook into the next chain or stitch and yarn over. Pull the yarn through the chain or stitch. You will have 2 loops on your hook.

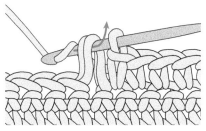

2 Yarn over and pull yarn through both loops on your hook to complete the single crochet.

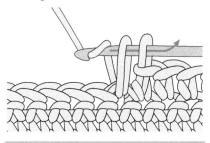

## Half Double Crochet (hdc)

1 Yarn over and insert your hook into the next chain or stitch. Yarn over a 2nd time and pull the yarn through the chain or stitch. You will have 3 loops on your hook.

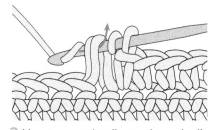

2 Yarn over and pull yarn through all 3 loops on your hook to complete the half double crochet.

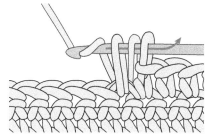

# CROCHET STITCHES ////

## Double Crochet (dc)

**1** Yarn over and insert your hook into the next chain or stitch. Yarn over a 2nd time and pull the yarn through the chain or stitch. You will have 3 loops on your hook.

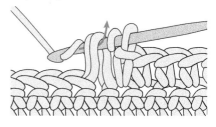

**2** Yarn over and pull yarn through just the first 2 loops on your hook. You will have 2 loops remaining on your hook.

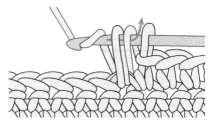

**3** Yarn over and pull yarn through the last 2 loops on your hook to complete the double crochet.

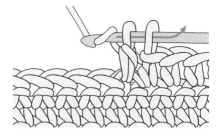

## Treble Crochet (tr)

**1** Yarn over 2 times and insert your hook into the next chain or stitch. Yarn over a 3rd time and pull the yarn through the chain or stitch. You will have 4 loops on your hook.

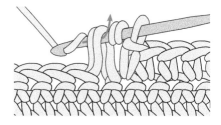

**2** Yarn over and pull yarn through the first 2 loops on your hook. You will have 3 loops remaining on your hook.

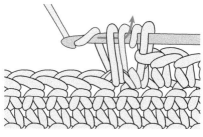

**3** Yarn over and pull yarn through the next 2 loops on your hook. You will have 2 loops remaining on your hook.

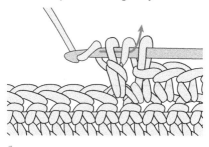

**4** Yarn over and pull yarn through the remaining 2 loops on your hook to finish the treble crochet.

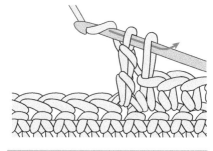

## Front Post Single Crochet (FPsc)

**1** Insert your hook below your next stitch to the right of the stitch's post. Work the hook around the post from front to back to front again and yarn over.

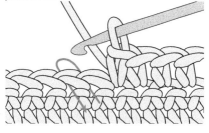

**2** Pull the yarn around the back of the post. You will have 2 loops on your hook. Yarn over and pull yarn through both loops on your hook to finish the stitch.

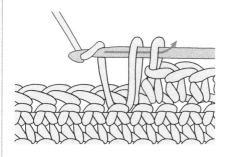

## Back Post Single Crochet (BPsc)

**1** Starting behind your work, insert your hook below your next stitch to the right of the stitch's post. Work the hook around the post from back to front to back again and yarn over.

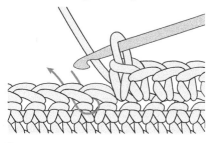

**2** Pull the yarn around the front of the post. You will have 2 loops on the hook. Yarn over and pull yarn through both loops on the hook to finish the stitch.

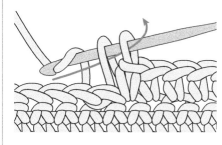

You can also work around the post using other stitches like half double crochet (FPhdc/BPhdc) or double crochet (FPdc/BPdc).

## Increases (sc 2 in next st)

Work 2 or more stitches into the same stitch when indicated.

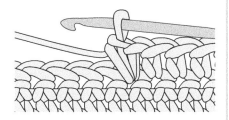

## Decreases

Patterns in this book use a variety of decrease options, such as crocheting 2 to 3 stitches together and/or skipping stitches entirely.

## Skip (sk)

Per the pattern instructions, count and skip the number of stitches indicated before working the next stitch in the pattern.

## Single-Crochet Decrease (sc2tog)

1 Insert your hook into the next stitch, yarn over the hook, and pull through the stitch, leaving a loop on your hook. You'll have 2 loops on your hook.

2 Repeat step 1 in the next stitch. You'll have 3 loops on your hook.

3 Yarn over the hook and pull through all 3 loops. You'll have 1 loop on your hook.

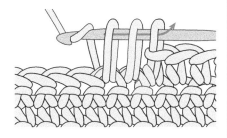

## Half-Double Crochet Decrease (Hdc2tog)

Yarn over first and then proceed to step 1. You will have 3 loops on your hook. Yarn over again and proceed to step 2. You will have 5 loops on your hook. Yarn over and pull yarn through all loops on hook to complete the decrease.

## Double Crochet Decrease (dc2tog)

Yarn over first and then proceed to step 1. You will have 3 loops on your hook. Yarn over again and proceed to step 2. You will have 5 loops on your hook. Yarn over and pull yarn through the first 4 loops on hook so 2 loops remain. Yarn over and pull yarn through remaining 2 loops to complete the decrease.

## Single Crochet 3 Together (sc3tog)

Keep repeating step 2 until you have 4 loops on your hook. Proceed to yarn over and pull the hook through all loops to complete the decrease.

## Single Crochet 4 Together (sc4tog)

Keep repeating step 2 until you have 5 loops on your hook. Proceed to yarn over and pull the hook through all loops to complete the decrease.

## Invisible Single-Crochet Decrease (sc2tog)

This technique can be used instead of the standard single-crochet decrease. It helps eliminate the gaps that can sometimes occur when using the standard single-crochet decrease.

1 Insert your hook into the front loop of the next stitch and then immediately into the front loop of the following stitch. You will have 3 loops on your hook.

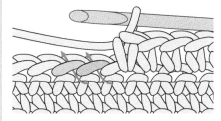

2 Yarn over and draw the working yarn through the 2 front loops on the hook. You'll have 2 loops on your hook.

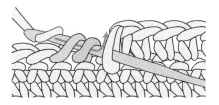

3 Yarn over the hook and pull through both loops on your hook to complete the stitch. You'll have 1 loop on your hook.

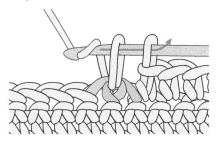

For an invisible half double crochet decrease (hdc2tog), yarn over first and then proceed to decrease as written for the single-crochet decrease until you have 3 loops on your hook. Yarn over and draw through all 3 loops to complete the stitch.

## Working in Back Loops (bl), Front Loops (fl), and Both Loops (tbl)

Unless otherwise noted, work in both loops of a stitch except when the pattern instructs that a stitch should be worked in the back loop or front loop. The front loop is the loop closest to you. The back loop is behind the front loop. If a round or row begins with "In bl" or "In fl," work entire round/row in that manner unless you are instructed to switch.

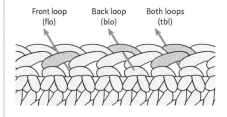

Front loop (flo)    Back loop (blo)    Both loops (tbl)

# CROCHET TECHNIQUES

## Working in Rows

Work the pattern until you reach the end of your row. Turn your work. Before beginning your next row, you will be asked to make a turning chain per the pattern instructions. Once your chain is completed, skip the turning chain and insert your hook into the first stitch in your new row and continue working the pattern.

## Working in the Round

Many patterns in this book are worked in a spiral round in which there are no slip stitches or chains between rounds. When you reach the end of the round, simply continue crocheting into the next. If needed, use a place marker to help keep track of where your rounds begin and end.

## Adjustable Ring (AR)

The adjustable ring is a great technique that will minimize the hole in the middle of your starting round.
1 Form a ring with your yarn, leaving a 6" tail to work with. Insert the hook into the loop as if you were making a slipknot.

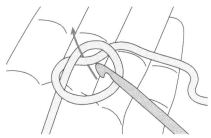

2 Yarn over the hook and pull through the loop to make a slip stitch, but do not tighten the loop.

3 Chain 1 and then single crochet over both strands of yarn that make up the edge of the adjustable ring until you've reached the number of stitches indicated in the pattern. To close the center of the ring, pull firmly on the yarn tail.

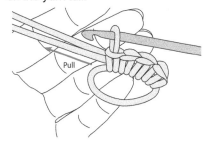

Pull

To start your next round, work your next stitch in the first single crochet of the completed adjustable ring. For patterns that require a semi-circle base shape, you will be asked to turn the work so that the back of the piece faces you before you make a turning chain and begin working the next row in your pattern.

## Working in a Chain Space (ch sp)

Proceed with making your next stitch as you normally would, but in this instance, work your stitches into the space below the chain.

## Right Side (RS)/Wrong Side (WS)

When working in the round, the side of your pattern perceived as the "right side" will affect which part of the stitch is the back loop versus the front loop. The 6-inch (15cm) tail left over from forming the adjustable ring will usually be on the wrong side of the piece. The same can be said for patterns that begin by working around a chain, provided you hold the 6-inch (15cm) yarn tail at the back of your work as you crochet the first round.

## Changing Colors

Work the stitch before the color change up until the last step in which you would normally draw the yarn through the loop(s) on your hook to complete the stitch.

To change colors, yarn over the hook with your new color and draw the new color through the remaining loop(s) on your hook, completing the stitch. You can then continue on to the next stitch in the new color.

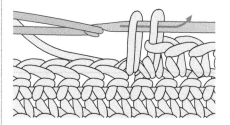

For color changes at the beginning of a new row, complete the stitch in your previous row and turn your work. Introduce the new color when you make your turning chain. Continue to work with your new color for the next row.

For color changes that take place in a slip stitch, simply insert the hook into the old color stitch, yarn over with the new color, and draw the new color through the loop on your hook to complete your slip stitch and the color change.

## Working Around a Chain

When working around a chain of stitches, you'll first work in the back ridge loops of the chain and then in the front side of the chain to create your first round.
1 Make a chain per the pattern instructions. To begin round 1, work your first stitch in the back ridge loop of the 2nd chain from your hook. Mark this stitch with a place marker to make it easier to find when you are ready to begin round 2. Work the rest of the stitches indicated into the back ridge loops of the chain until you've reached the last chain above the

slipknot. Work the indicated number of stitches into the back ridge loop of this last chain.

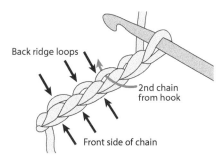

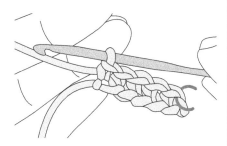

**2** When you're ready to work the other side of the chain, rotate your work so the front side of the chain faces up. Starting in the next chain, insert your hook under the front side of the chain to work your next stitch.

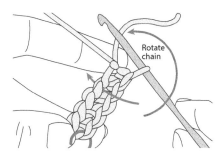

**3** Continue working in the front sides of the remaining chains. Once the round is complete, continue on to round 2 (indicated by your stitch marker).

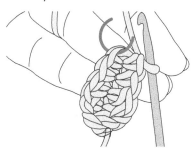

## Surface Loops

Working in just the front loop or back loop of a stitch will create a line of surface loops on your work. These lines of raised stitches often serve as landmarks when your work needs to be folded or bent and will usually remain visible on the right side of your finished work. Look for references to surface loops on the assembly illustrations represented by a line of closely spaced stitches.

## Working in Surface Loops

This technique will usually be worked in raised loops that will be visible after you've worked a round in the back loops of your stitches or in the front posts.

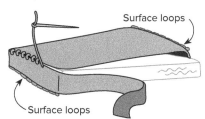

**1** Begin by locating which round you will be working in. Insert your hook under the exposed loop(s) on the surface of your work. Rejoin your yarn with a yarn over and pull the yarn through the surface stitch.

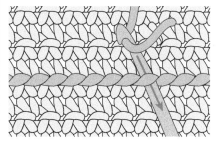

Exposed front loops from working bl sc sts

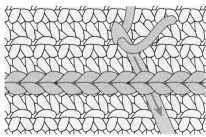

Exposed loops from working FPsc sts

**2** Chain 1 and apply a stitch (like a single crochet) into the same surface loop you started in. This will create your first surface stitch.

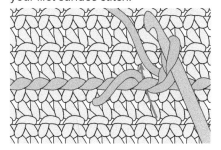

You can then continue to work in the remaining surface stitches in the round.

## Twisted Cords

Perfect for rope details! Cut a length of yarn 4 to 6 times longer than your finished cord will be. Holding the cut ends in one hand, take the folded end in your other hand and catch the loop on your finger. Spin/rotate your finger to twist the yarn.

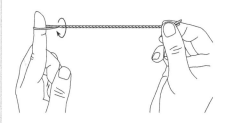

Continue to twist until the yarn twists and doubles over on itself. Measure out the final length of cord needed and tie the folded and cut ends together in a square knot to secure the twist.

# FINISHING STITCHES

Once your pattern pieces are complete, you can assemble and embellish your construction fleet with just a handful of basic stitches. To ensure all the final details end up in the right spots, look over the photos for each vehicle before you begin assembling them and use marking pins to help you work out the placement of your pattern pieces before sewing them together.

> Leave long yarn tails when you fasten off the last rounds of your pieces. When assembling, use marking pins to test-fit the pieces together to ensure everything is even and balanced. Then, using the leftover yarn tails, place a single stitch at each marking pin to hold your pieces in place. Remove the pins and finish sewing your pieces down using a whip or mattress stitch.

## Whip Stitch

Use this stitch to close flat seams. Hold the edges of your work together and, using your tapestry needle and yarn, draw the yarn through the edges before looping the yarn over the top of your work and back through the edges again in a spiral-like motion. Continue until the seam is closed or the piece is attached.

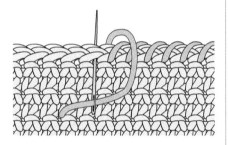

## Mattress Stitch

The mattress stitch provides a nice tight seam when sewing crochet surfaces together.

Choose a point on the surface or edge of your first piece and insert the needle from A to B under a single stitch and pull the yarn through.

Cross over to the opposite surface and draw your needle under a single stitch from C to D with the entry point at C lining up between points A and B on the first surface. Return to the first surface and insert your needle directly next to exit point

B. Continue to work back and forth in this manner until seam is closed, pulling firmly after every few stitches to ensure a clean, closed seam.

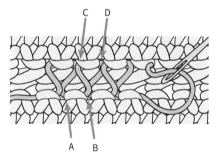

## Closing Round Holes

For closing round holes like the ones at the last rounds of tires, start by threading the remaining yarn tail onto a tapestry needle. Following the edge of the round opening, insert the needle through just the front loops of each stitch, effectively winding the yarn tail around the front loops of the stitches. When you've worked all the way around the opening, pull the tail firmly to close the hole (just like you were cinching a drawstring bag closed).

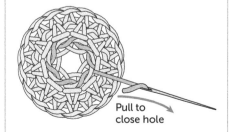

Pull to close hole

## Running Stitch

Use this stitch to attach felt pieces or flattened crochet pieces to your work. To apply this stitch, draw your yarn or thread in and out of the surface(s) of your piece in a dashed line pattern.

## Back Stitch

Use this stitch to create line details on the surface of your piece. Begin by drawing the yarn up through the surface of your piece at A and then reinsert the needle at B. Next, draw your yarn up at C and then reinsert the needle at A.

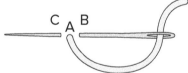

Continue to work in this manner to create a solid line of stitches.

## Chain Stitch

1 Start by making a small stitch on the surface of your work. Bring the needle up through your work about a stitch length away, pass the needle through the small stitch, and reinsert the needle into its starting point.  This is your first chain.

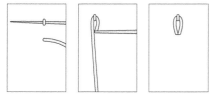

2 Bring your needle up through your work a stitch below your last chain. Slide the needle under your last chain and reinsert the needle into its starting point. Repeat.

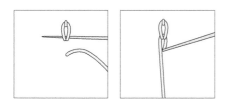

Try this trick to reduce the hassle of dealing with yarn ends when adding embroidery details!

Begin by inserting your needle about an inch from where you intend to start your embroidery stitch and leave a 4-inch (10cm) tail. Bring the needle up at the first stitch. Hold the yarn tail down with your fingers as you work the first couple of stitches until the yarn appears to feel secure. When you finish your last stitch, bring the needle out at the same spot of the beginning tail and cut the end, leaving another 4-inch (10cm) tail. Knot the 2 yarn tails together, and then use a crochet hook or tapestry needle to draw the yarn and the knot back through the hole with a firm tug. Trim any visible yarn tails if needed.

# FLATBED TRUCK

**FINISHED SIZE:** 16 x 8 x 6½ in. (41 x 20 x 17cm)  **YARN WEIGHT:**

This versatile truck with a generous flatbed and chunky tires will help keep things moving in and out of any construction site. This pattern works perfectly as a stand-alone truck or can be modified with a working dumper (page 23) or spinning cement drum (page 28).

(page 23) ... (page 28)

## MATERIALS & TOOLS

- Bulky-weight yarn in black (100 yds/91m), light gray (450 yds/412m), purple (150 yds/137m), and white (100 yds/91m)
- Hook size I (5.5mm)
- Tapestry needle
- Scissors
- Polyester fiberfill
- 1-in. (25mm)-thick cushion foam

## INSTRUCTIONS

### TRUCK CAB SIDE (MAKE 2)

**TIP:** To create a driver's side and passenger's side, switch which side of the pattern the leftover yarn tails lie on your color change rows when you construct your second piece.

Starting with purple, loosely ch 20.

**Row 1:** Starting in 2nd ch from hook and working in back ridge loops, sc 19, turn. (19 sts)

**Rows 2–8:** Ch 1, sc 19, turn. (19 sts)

**Row 9:** Ch 1, sc 17, sc2tog, turn. (18 sts)

**Row 10:** Ch 1, sc2tog, sc 16, turn. (17 sts)

**Row 11:** Ch 1, sc 2, cut yarn, leaving a 48-inch (1.2m) tail to work with, change to white, sc 7, rejoin purple from skein, sc 2 and leave remaining sts unworked. Turn. (11 sts)

# FLATBED TRUCK ////

**Rows 12–14:** Ch 1, sc 2, change to white, sc 7, change to purple, sc 2, turn. (11 sts)

**Row 15:** Ch 1, sc 2, change to white, sc 6, change to purple, sc 1, sc2tog, turn. (10 sts)

**Row 16:** Ch 1, sc 2, change to white, sc 6, change to purple, sc 2, turn. (10 sts)

Cut white.

**Row 17:** Ch 1, sc 8, sc2tog, turn. (9 sts)

**Row 18:** Ch 1, sc2tog, sc 7. (8 sts)

Cut yarn and fasten off, leaving a long tail for sewing.

## TRUCK CAB CENTER

Starting with purple, loosely ch 16.

**Row 1:** Starting in 2nd ch from hook and working in back ridge loops, sc 15, turn. (15 sts)

**Rows 2–10:** Ch 1, sc 15, turn. (15 sts)

**Row 11:** Ch 1, in bl; sc2tog, sc 11, sc2tog, turn. (13 sts)

**Row 12:** Ch 1, sc2tog, sc 9, sc2tog, turn. (11 sts)

**Rows 13–16:** Ch 1, sc 11, turn. (11 sts)

**Row 17:** Ch 1, sc 2 in next st, sc 9, sc 2 in next st, turn. (13 sts)

**Row 18:** Keep yarn tails on front side of work for row 18. Ch 1, bl; sc 1, cut purple leaving a 48-inch (1.2m) tail to work with, change to white, sc 2 in next st, sc 9, sc 2 in next st, rejoin purple yarn from skein, sc 1, turn. (15 sts)

**Rows 19–21:** Ch 1, sc 1, change to white, sc 13, change to purple, sc 1, turn. (15 sts)

**Row 22:** Ch 1, sc 1, change to white, sc2tog, sc 9, sc2tog, change to purple, sc 1, turn. (13 sts)

**Row 23:** Ch 1, sc 1, change to white, sc 11, change to purple, sc 1, turn. (13 sts)

Cut white.

**Row 24:** Ch 1, sc2tog, sc 9, sc2tog, turn. (11 sts)

**Row 25:** Ch 1, sc 11, turn. (11 sts)

**Row 26:** Ch 1, in fl; sc 11, turn. (11 sts)

**Rows 27–33:** Ch 1, sc 11, turn. (11 sts)

**Row 34:** Ch 1, in fl; sc 11, turn. (11 sts)

**Row 35:** Ch 1, sc 11, turn. (11 sts)

**Row 36:** Keep yarn tails on front side of work for row 36. Ch 1, sc 1, cut purple leaving a 48-inch (1.2m) tail

to work with, change to white, sc 9, rejoin purple yarn from skein, sc 1, turn. (11 sts)

**Rows 37–41:** Ch 1, sc 1, change to white, sc 9, change to purple, sc 1, turn. (11 sts)

Cut white.

**Rows 42–45:** Ch 1, sc 11, turn. (11 sts)

**Row 46:** Ch 1, sc 2 in next st, sc 9, sc 2 in next st, turn. (13 sts)

**Rows 47–48:** Ch 1, sc 13, turn. (13 sts)

**Row 49:** Ch 1, sc 2 in next st, sc 11, sc 2 in next st, turn. (15 sts)

**Rows 50–51:** Ch 1, sc 15, turn. (15 sts)

**Row 52:** Ch 1, in fl; sc 15, turn. (15 sts)

**Rows 53–69:** Ch 1, sc 15, turn. (15 sts)

**Row 70:** Ch 1, sc 15. (15 sts)

Cut yarn and fasten off, leaving a long tail for sewing.

Match up one cab side with the cab center and pin or use slip rings to hold the edges together. Sew edges. Rep on the other side. Stuff the cab with fiberfill through the front opening below the hood before closing seam.

With purple, draw a line of running stitches between the base of the windshield and the bottom of the cab, pulling gently to shape the hood.

Double up light gray yarn on a tapestry needle and embroider a chain stitch around the side and back windows, as well as the side and top edges of the windshield (see photos).

## FRONT BUMPER

Using light gray, loosely ch 19.

**Row 1:** Starting in 2nd ch from hook and working in back ridge loops, sc 18, turn. (18 sts)

**Rows 2–8:** Ch 1, sc 18, turn. (18 sts)

Cut yarn and fasten off, leaving a long tail for sewing.

Fold the long way and whip stitch first and last rows tog. Flatten bumper with seam in back and sew the

short edges closed. Wrap the front of the bumper around the front and side corners of the truck cab and sew in place.

## GRILL

Using light gray, loosely ch 11.

**Row 1:** Starting in 2nd chain from hook, sc 10, turn. (10 sts)

**Row 2:** Ch 1, sl st 10 loosely, turn. (10 sts)

**Row 3:** Ch 1, sc 10, turn. (10 sts)

**Rows 4–7:** Rep rows 2–3 2 more times.

**Row 8:** Ch 1, sl st 10. (10 sts)

Cont to sl st around outside edges of the grill until you have reached the other side of row 8.

Cut yarn and fasten off, leaving a long tail for sewing.

Sew the grill to the front of the truck above the bumper.

## HEADLIGHTS (MAKE 2)

Starting with white, make a 4-st adjustable ring.

**Rnd 1:** (Sl st, sc 1, sl st) in each st around. (12 sts)

Change to light gray.

**Rnd 2:** In bl; sl st 12.

Cut yarn and fasten off, leaving a long tail for sewing.

Sew headlights to front of truck next to the upper corners of the grill.

## FRONT CAB TIRES (MAKE 2)

Using black, make a 6-st adjustable ring.

**Rnd 1:** Sc 2 in each st around. (12 sts)

**Rnd 2:** *Sc 1, sc 2 in next st; rep from * 5 more times. (18 sts)

**Rnd 3:** *Sc 2, sc 2 in next st; rep from * 5 more times. (24 sts)

**Rnd 4:** *Sc 3, sc 2 in next st; rep from * 5 more times. (30 sts)

**Rnds 5–6:** Sc 30. (30 sts)

**Rnd 7:** *Sc 3, sc2tog; rep from * 5 more times. (24 sts)

**Rnd 8:** *Sc 2, sc2tog; rep from * 5 more times. (18 sts)

**Rnd 9:** *Sc 1, sc2tog; rep from * 5 more times. (12 sts)

Stuff tire.

**Rnd 10:** Sc2tog 6 times. (6 sts)

Fasten off yarn, leaving a long tail for sewing. Close the 6-st hole.

Thread the yarn tail back and forth through the center of the tire 3 to 4 times, pulling tightly as you sew to shape the tire.

## FRONT CAB TIRE HUBCAP (MAKE 2)

Using light gray, make a 6-st adjustable ring.

**Rnd 1:** Sc 2 in each st around. (12 sts)

Cut yarn and fasten off, leaving a long tail for sewing.

Sew hubcaps onto the center of the tires.

## FRONT FENDER (MAKE 2)

Using purple, make a 6-st adjustable ring.

**Rnd 1:** Sc 2 in each st around. (12 sts)

**Rnds 2–16:** Sc 12. (12 sts)

**Rnd 17:** Sc2tog 6 times. (6 sts)

Fasten off yarn, leaving a long tail for sewing. Close the 6-st hole.

Wrap the front fenders over the top of the tires and secure to the sides and top of the tire with a few stitches. Sew front tires onto the sides of the cab. Sew the inside edge of the fender to the side of the cab.

## TRUCK BED TIRE (MAKE 4)

Using black, make a 6-st adjustable ring.

**Rnd 1:** Sc 2 in each st around. (12 sts)

**Rnd 2:** *Sc 1, sc 2 in next st; rep from * 5 more times. (18 sts)

**Rnd 3:** *Sc 2, sc 2 in next st; rep from * 5 more times. (24 sts)

**Rnds 4–5:** Sc 24. (24 sts)

**Rnd 6:** *Sc 2, sc2tog; rep from * 5 more times. (18 sts)

**Rnd 7:** *Sc 1, sc2tog; rep from * 5 more times. (12 sts)

Stuff tire.

**Rnd 8:** Sc2tog 6 times. (6 sts)

Fasten off yarn, leaving a long tail for sewing. Close the 6-st hole.

Thread the yarn tail back and forth through the center of the tire 3 to 4 times, pulling tightly as you sew to shape the tire.

## TRUCK BED TIRE HUBCAPS (MAKE 4)

Using light gray, make a 4-st adjustable ring.

**Rnd 1:** Sc 2 in each st around. (8 sts)

Cut yarn and fasten off, leaving a long tail for sewing.

Sew the hubcaps to the sides of the tires.

## TRUCK BED

Using light gray, loosely ch 68.

**Row 1:** Starting in 2nd ch from hook, sc 67, turn. (67 sts)

**Rows 2–3:** Ch 1, sc 67, turn. (67 sts)

Cut yarn and fasten off, leaving a long tail for sewing.

**Row 4:** Count 27 sts in from end. Work (sl st 1, ch 1, sc 1) in fl of 27th st (counts as first st). Cont to work in fl; sc 14 and leave remaining sts unworked. Turn. (15 sts)

**Rows 5–34:** Ch 1, sc 15, turn. (15 sts)

**Row 35:** Ch 1, in bl; sc 15, turn. (15 sts)

**Rows 36–37:** Ch 1, sc 15, turn. (15 sts)

**Row 38:** Ch 1, in fl; sc 15, turn. (15 sts)

**Rows 39–68:** Ch 1, sc 15, turn. (15 sts)

Cut yarn and fasten off, leaving a long tail for sewing.

Cut 1-inch (25mm) cushion foam into (1) 8 x 4¼-inch (20 x 11cm) rectangle. With the surface loops of the truck bed facing out, insert foam between the top and bottom layers of the truck bed. Pin or use slip rings to hold side edges in place. With light gray yarn, sew edges together with a whip stitch.

**Rows 6–7:** Ch 1, sc 28, turn. (28 sts)

**Row 8:** Ch 1, in fl; sc 28, turn. (28 sts)

**Row 9:** Ch 1, in bl; sc 28, turn. (28 sts)

**Row 10:** Ch 1, sc 28, turn. (28 sts)

**Row 11:** Ch 1, sc 28. (28 sts)

Cut yarn and fasten off, leaving a long tail for sewing.

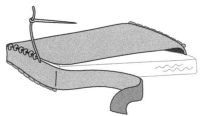

Sew one short end of the truck bed to the back of the truck cab.

## TRUCK BED DOUBLE WHEEL WELL (MAKE 2)

Using light gray, loosely ch 19.

**Row 1:** Starting in 2nd ch from hook, sc 18, turn. (18 sts)

**Row 2:** Ch 1, sc 18, turn. (18 sts)

**Row 3:** Ch 1, sl st 1, sc 1, hdc 14, sc, sl st 1, turn. (18 sts)

**Row 4:** Ch 1, sl st 1, sc 1, hdc 1, dc 12, hdc 1, sc 1, sl st 1. (18 sts)

Cut yarn and fasten off, leaving a long tail for sewing. (Sl st 1, ch 1, sc 2) in the right corner of row 1 (counts as first 2 stitches of row 5) and proceed to work around the edge of the piece as follows:

**Row 5:** Sc 3 along the edge of rows 1–4. In fl of row 4; sc 18. Sc 3, sc 2 in last st along the edge of rows 4–1, turn. (28 sts)

Fold row 11 back to row 8 and whip stitch together to create the wheel well fender. The surface loops from rows 10 and 11 should be facing out. Flatten and whip stitch the ends of the fender shut.

Position one of the wheel wells along the side edge of the truck bed. Whip stitch the bottom edge of the wheel well to the bottom edge of the truck bed side. Apply more stitches along the top edge of the truck bed and the back wall of the wheel well to hold everything in place. Rep on the other side.

Attach two truck bed tires side by side into the wheel well. If desired, apply a few stitches of light gray between the sides and tops of the tires and the inside of the wheel well fender to keep the fender lying flat.

Weave in any remaining yarn tails.

# DUMP TRUCK

**FINISHED SIZE:** 14 x 7 x 6 in. (36 x 18 x 15cm) /// **YARN WEIGHT:**

**D**ump truck has great details like a tipping dumper and working tailgate. Don't forget to make a whole pile of rocks (page 110) to fill up the back, or else you might find your yarn skeins being hauled about instead (speaking from experience!).

## INSTRUCTIONS

### TRUCK

Make Flatbed Truck (page 16) as instructed, replacing purple yarn with green yarn.

### DUMPER

Using dark gray, loosely ch 12.

**Rnd 1:** Starting in 2nd ch and working in back ridge loops, sc 10, sc 4 in next ch. Rotate chain so front side of chain is facing up. Starting in front side of the next ch, sc 9, sc 3 in front side of next ch. (26 sts)

**Rnd 2:** Sc 3 in next st, sc 9, sc 3 in next st, sc 2, sc 3 in next st, sc 9, sc 3 in next st, sc 2. (34 sts)

**Rnd 3:** Sc 1, sc 3 in next st, sc 11, sc 3 in next st, sc 4, sc 3 in next st, sc 11, sc 3 in next st, sc 3. (42 sts)

**Rnd 4:** Sc 2, sc 3 in next st, sc 13, sc 3 in next st, sc 6, sc 3 in next st, sc 13, sc 3 in next st, sc 4. (50 sts)

**Rnd 5:** Sc 3, sc 3 in next st, sc 15, sc 3 in next st, sc 8, sc 3 in next st, sc 15, sc 3 in next st, sc 5. (58 sts)

**Rnd 6:** Sc 4, sc 3 in next st, sc 17, sc 3 in next st, sc 10, sc 3 in next st, sc 17, sc 3 in next st, sc 6. (66 sts)

**Rnd 7:** Sc 5, sc 3 in next st, sc 19, sc 3 in next st, sc 12, sc 3 in next st, sc 19, sc 3 in next st, sc 7. (74 sts)

### Dumper floor flap
To begin: Sl st 6, turn.

**Row 1:** Ch 1, in fl; sc 14. Count 2 sts ahead of hook and pm. Turn work. (14 sts)

**Row 2:** Ch 1, in bl; sc 14, turn. (14 sts)

**Rows 3–26:** Ch 1, sc 14, turn. (14 sts)

Cut yarn and fasten off, leaving a long tail for sewing.

### Side wall 1
**Row 1:** (Sl st, ch 1, sc 1) in fl of pm stitch to re-attach yarn. Cont working in fl; sc 20. Count 2 sts ahead of hook and pm. Turn work. (21 sts)

**Rows 2–8:** Ch 1, sc 21, turn. (21 sts)

**Rows 9–10:** Ch 1, in bl; sc 21, turn. (21 sts)

**Row 11:** Ch 1, in fl; sc 21, turn. (21 sts)

**Row 12:** Ch 1, sc 21, turn. (21 sts)

**Row 13:** Ch 1, in fl; sc 21, turn. (21 sts)

**Rows 14–20:** Ch 1, sc 21, turn. (21 sts)

Cut yarn and fasten off, leaving a long tail for sewing.

### Back wall
**Row 1:** (Sl st, ch 1, sc 1) in fl of pm stitch to re-attach yarn. Cont working in fl; sc 13. Count 2 sts ahead of hook and pm. Turn work. (14 sts)

**Rows 2–12:** Ch 1, sc 14, turn. (14 sts)

(Begin canopy section)

**Row 13:** Ch 1, in bl; sc 14, turn. (14 sts)

**Rows 14–15:** Ch 1, sc 14, turn. (14 sts)

**Row 16:** Ch 1, in bl; sc 14, turn. (14 sts)

**Row 17:** Ch 1, in fl; sc 14, turn. (14 sts)

**Rows 18–21:** Ch 1, sc 14, turn. (14 sts)

**Row 22:** Ch 1, in bl; sc 14, turn. (14 sts)

(Canopy section of dumper wall complete)

**Rows 23–33:** Ch 1, sc 14, turn. (14 sts)

Cut yarn and fasten off, leaving a long tail for sewing.

### Side wall 2
Rep side wall 1 but do not pm.

## TAILGATE

With dark gray, loosely ch 14.

**Row 1:** Starting in 2nd ch from hook and working in back ridge loops, sc 13, turn.

# DUMP TRUCK ///

**Rows 2–7:** Ch 1, sc 13, turn. (13 sts)

**Rows 8–9:** Ch 1, in fl; sc 13, turn. (13 sts)

**Row 10:** Ch 1, in bl; sc 13, turn. (13 sts)

**Row 11:** Ch 1, sc 13, turn. (13 sts)

**Row 12:** Ch 1, in bl; sc 13, turn. (13 sts)

**Rows 13–18:** Ch 1, sc 13, turn. (13 sts)

Cut yarn and fasten off, leaving a long tail for sewing.

Using foam stabilizer, cut out the following pieces:

- (1) dumper floor: 6 x 3 ¼-inch (15 x 8cm)
- (2) side walls: 2 x 5 ¾-inch (5 x 15cm)
- (1) back wall shelf: 3 ¼ x 1 ¼-inch (8 x 3cm)
- (1) back wall: 3 ¼ x 3 ¼-inch (8 x 8cm)
- (1) tailgate: 3 x 1 ¾-inch (8 x 4cm)

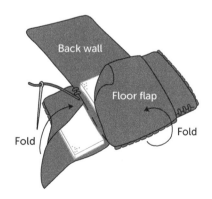

With WS of the dumper bed facing up (the yarn tail from rnd 1 is on this side), fold the dumper floor flap over the bed to match up the edges. Place the foam floor piece inside the floor and sew edges down. Fold over the side walls toward the center of the dumper and place the side foam pieces inside the walls. Sew bottom edges to floor of dumper and sew side edges closed.

Fold over the back wall toward the center of the dumper. Place the smaller back wall shelf foam piece

inside the upper canopy section of the back wall and the back wall foam piece inside the lower section. Sew the bottom edge of back wall to floor of dumper and sew side edges closed.

Sew a running stitch between the canopy section and the lower back wall section between the two pieces of foam.

Match up and sew the corner edges of the dumper walls together.

Fold first and last rows of tailgate tog with surface loops from rows 10 and 12 facing out. Insert tailgate foam inside tailgate and sew edges together. Sew top corners of tailgate to the top corners of the dumper sides, allowing the tailgate to swing.

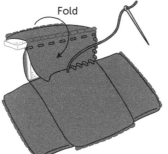

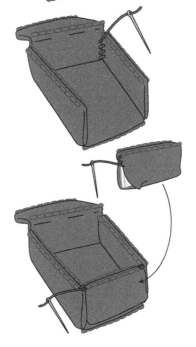

Double up dark gray yarn on tapestry needle and embroider 3 evenly spaced lines of chain stitches to each side of the dumper and 2 lines of chain stitches to the tailgate.

Sew the back edge of the dumper to the back edge of the truck bed to allow the dumper to tip.

Weave in any remaining yarn tails.

# CEMENT MIXER

**FINISHED SIZE:** 16 x 8 x 8½ in. (41 x 20 x 22cm)    **YARN WEIGHT:**

This cement mixer spins and is sure to be a big hit on the job site! Foam stabilizer is the secret to giving this cement drum its shaping while keeping all the huggability intact.

## INSTRUCTIONS

### TRUCK

Make Flatbed Truck (page 16) as instructed, replacing purple yarn with blue yarn.

### MIXING DRUM

Starting with white, loosely ch 28. Sl st to join last ch to first ch.

**Drum exterior**

**Rnd 1:** In back ridge loops of ch 28, sc 28. (28 sts)

**Rnd 2:** *Sc 6, sc 2 in next st; rep from * 3 more times. (32 sts)

**Rnd 3:** *Sc 7, sc 2 in next st; rep from * 3 more times. (36 sts)

**Rnd 4:** *Sc 8, sc 2 in next st; rep from * 3 more times. (40 sts)

**Rnd 5:** *Sc 9, sc 2 in next st; rep from * 3 more times. (44 sts)

**Rnd 6:** *Sc 10, sc 2 in next st; rep from * 3 more times. (48 sts)

**Rnd 7:** *Sc 11, sc 2 in next st; rep from * 3 more times. (52 sts)

**Rnd 8:** *Sc 12, sc 2 in next st; rep from * 3 more times. (56 sts)

**Rnd 9:** *Sc 13, sc 2 in next st; rep from * 3 more times. (60 sts)

**Rnd 10:** *Sc 14, sc 2 in next st; rep from * 3 more times. (64 sts)

**Rnd 11:** Sc 64. (64 sts)

Cut white.

**Rnds 12–19:** *Change to black, sc 4, change to yellow, sc 4; rep from * 7 more times.

**TIP:** When switching between colors, work color floats as loosely as possible. To avoid twisting the yarns as you work, pass yellow over the strand of black and black under the strand of yellow as you switch colors every time.

Cut yellow and black. Change to white.

**Rnd 20:** Sc 64. (64 sts)

**Rnd 21:** *Sc 14, sc2tog; rep from * 3 more times. (60 sts)

**Rnd 22:** *Sc 18, sc2tog; rep from * 2 more times. (57 sts)

**Rnd 23:** *Sc 17, sc2tog; rep from * 2 more times. (54 sts)

**Rnd 24:** *Sc 16, sc2tog; rep from * 2 more times. (51 sts)

**Rnd 25:** *Sc 15, sc2tog; rep from * 2 more times. (48 sts)

**Rnd 26:** *Sc 14, sc2tog; rep from * 2 more times. (45 sts)

**Rnd 27:** *Sc 13, sc2tog; rep from * 2 more times. (42 sts)

**Rnd 28:** *Sc 12, sc2tog; rep from * 2 more times. (39 sts)

**Rnd 29:** *Sc 11, sc2tog; rep from * 2 more times. (36 sts)

**Rnd 30:** *Sc 10, sc2tog; rep from * 2 more times. (33 sts)

**Rnd 31:** *Sc 9, sc2tog; rep from * 2 more times. (30 sts)

**Rnd 32:** *Sc 13, sc2tog; rep from * 1 more time. (28 sts)

**Rnd 33:** In bl; *sc 12, sc2tog; rep from * 1 more. (26 sts)

## Drum interior

**Rnd 34:** In bl; sc 26. (26 sts)

**Rnd 35:** *Sc 12, sc 2 in next st; rep from * 1 more time. (28 sts)

**Rnd 36:** *Sc 13, sc 2 in next st, rep from * 1 more time. (30 sts)

**Rnd 37:** *Sc 9, sc 2 in next st; rep from * 2 more times. (33 sts)

**Rnd 38:** *Sc 10, sc 2 in next st; rep from * 2 more times. (36 sts)

**Rnd 39:** *Sc 11, sc 2 in next st; rep from * 2 more times. (39 sts)

**Rnd 40:** *Sc 12, sc 2 in next st; rep from * 2 more times. (42 sts)

**Rnd 41:** *Sc 13, sc 2 in next st; rep from * 2 more times. (45 sts)

**Rnd 42:** *Sc 14, sc 2 in next st; rep from * 2 more times. (48 sts)

**Rnd 43:** *Sc 15, sc 2 in next st; rep from * 2 more times. (51 sts)

**Rnd 44:** *Sc 16, sc 2 in next st; rep from * 2 more times. (54 sts)

**Rnd 45:** *Sc 17, sc 2 in next st; rep from * 2 more times. (57 sts)

**Rnd 46:** *Sc 18, sc 2 in next st; rep from * 2 more times. (60 sts)

**Rnds 47–55:** Sc 60. (60 sts)

**Rnd 56:** *Sc 13, sc2tog; rep from * 3 more times. (56 sts)

**Rnd 57:** *Sc 12, sc2tog; rep from * 3 more times. (52 sts)

**Rnd 58:** *Sc 11, sc2tog; rep from * 3 more times. (48 sts)

**Rnd 59:** *Sc 10, sc2tog; rep from * 3 more times. (44 sts)

**Rnd 60:** *Sc 9, sc2tog; rep from * 3 more times. (40 sts)

**Rnd 61:** *Sc 8, sc2tog; rep from * 3 more times. (36 sts)

**Rnd 62:** *Sc 7, sc2tog; rep from * 3 more times. (32 sts)

**Rnd 63:** *Sc 6, sc2tog; rep from * 3 more times. (28 sts)

**Rnd 64:** *Sc 5, sc2tog; rep from * 3 more times. (24 sts)

**Rnd 65:** FPsc 24. (24 sts)

**Rnd 66:** *Sc 2, sc2tog; rep from * 5 more times. (18 sts)

**Rnd 67:** *Sc 1, sc2tog; rep from * 5 more times. (12 sts)

**Rnd 68:** Sc2tog 6 times. (6 sts)

Fasten off yarn and close hole.

Using foam stabilizer, cut (1) 18 x 8½-inch (46 x 22 cm) rectangle.

Along the long edges, make a mark every ½ inch (13mm). Along short edges, make a mark at 3½ inches (9cm), and 2 inches (5cm) beyond that. Connect these marks with two straight horizontal lines. There will now be three sections to the foam—a 3½-inch (9cm)

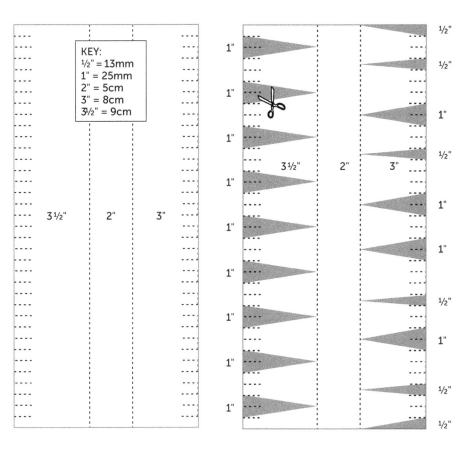

KEY:
½" = 13mm
1" = 25mm
2" = 5cm
3" = 8cm
3½" = 9cm

section, a 2-inch (5cm) section, and a 3-inch (8cm) section.

In the 3½-inch (9cm) and 3-inch (8cm) sections, cut darts per the illustration (indicated in gray).

With needle and thread, sew the 8½-inch (22cm) edges together to form a tube, then sew 1 to 2 stitches at the end of each dart to close the shaping. It's not necessary to sew the entire edge of each dart together—just a stitch or two at the end will suffice.

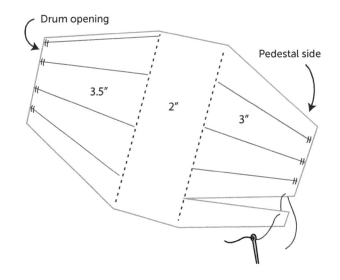

# CEMENT MIXER ////

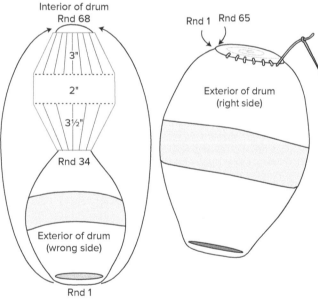

Turn piece inside out and slide the finished drum foam over the interior portion of the drum. The edge of the 3-inch (8cm) section of foam will line up with rnd 68 of the drum interior and the edge of the 3½-inch (9cm) section will line up around rnd 34 in the middle of the piece. Fold back the exterior section of the drum mixer over the interior section so as to sandwich the foam between the two layers. Use your hands to adjust and smooth of the foam between the layers.

Match up and sew rnd 65 to rnd 1.

## DRUM COVER

With white, make a 6-st adjustable ring.

**Rnd 1:** Sc 2 in each st around. (12 sts)

**Rnd 2:** *Sc 1, sc 2 in next st; rep from * 5 more times. (18 sts)

**Rnd 3:** *Sc 2, sc 2 in next st; rep from * 5 more times. (24 sts)

**Rnd 4:** *Sc 3, sc 2 in next st; rep from * 5 more times. (30 sts)

Cut yarn and fasten off, leaving a long tail for sewing.

From plastic canvas, cut out (1) 2¼-inch (6cm) circle. Sew it to the closed end of the drum with a few stitches. Cover the plastic circle with the drum cover and sew down the edge.

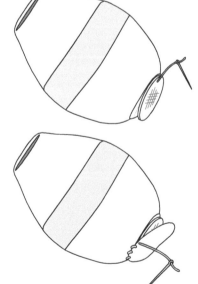

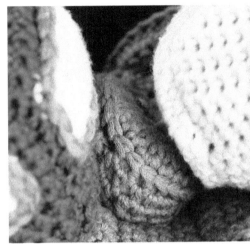

## DRUM PEDESTAL

With light gray, make a 6-st adjustable ring.

**Rnd 1:** Sc 2 in each st around. (12 sts)

**Rnd 2:** *Sc 1, sc 2 in next st; rep from * 5 more times. (18 sts)

**Rnd 3:** *Sc 2, sc 2 in next st; rep from * 5 more times. (24 sts)

**Rnd 4:** BPsc 24. (24 sts)

**Rnds 5–7:** Sl st 4, sc 3, hdc 3, dc 4, hdc 3, sc 3, sl st 4. (24 sts)

Cut yarn and fasten off, leaving a long tail for sewing.

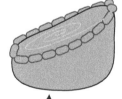

Cut (1) 2-inch (5cm) circle from plastic canvas and place it inside the pedestal. Apply a few stitches in light gray yarn to hold plastic in place.

Place open edge of pedestal against the floor of the truck bed with the taller side of the pedestal next to the back of the cab's rear wall. Sew open edge to truck bed, catching the foam as you sew for added

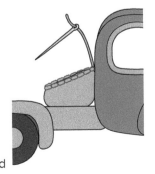

stability. Stuff pedestal firmly before closing seam. Tack taller side of pedestal to the back of the cab wall with a few stitches.

Attach a piece of light gray yarn to the underside of the truck in the center of the line where the cab meets the truck bed. Draw the yarn up through the truck bed and the center of the pedestal. Position the end of the drum against the pedestal and draw the yarn up through the drum end. Once the yarn is secured on the inside of the drum, draw the yarn

back out through the end of the drum, then take care to thread the yarn through the original path through the center of the pedestal and truck bed, back down to the point where the yarn was initially secured. Pull very tightly and secure yarn at the starting point.

Weave in any remaining yarn tails.

# FRONT LOADER

**FINISHED SIZE:** 13½ x 7 x 7 in. (34 x 18 x 18cm)  /// **YARN WEIGHT:**

Front loader is ready to clean up the biggest, rockiest jobs you can throw its way! With a generous front bucket that can lift and tilt, no job is too big for this mighty machine. To make your front loader into a backhoe, be sure to check out the excavator arm attachment on page 49.

## INSTRUCTIONS

**TIP:** Need something tough for the work site down on the farm? Try replacing the yellow yarn with green and skip the bucket attachments for a rough-and-tumble tractor!

### FRONT LOADER BASE

Using yellow, loosely ch 71.

**Row 1:** Starting in 2nd ch from hook, sc 70, turn. (70 sts)

**Rows 2–3:** Ch 1, sc 70, turn. (70 sts)

Cut yarn and fasten off, leaving a long tail for sewing. Turn work.

**Row 4:** Count 31 sts in from end. Working in fl of 31st st (sl st 1, ch 1, sc 1). Cont to work in fl; sc 9 and leave remaining sts unworked. Turn. (10 sts)

**Rows 5–11:** Ch 1, sc 10, turn. (10 sts)

**Row 12:** Ch 4. Starting in 2nd ch from hook, sc 3, sc 10, turn. (13 sts)

# FRONT LOADER ////

**Row 13:** Ch 4. Starting in 2nd ch from hook, sc 3, sc 13, turn. (16 sts)

**Rows 14–15:** Ch 1, sc 16, turn. (16 sts)

**Row 16:** Ch 1, sl st 3, sc 13, turn. (13 sts)

**Row 17:** Ch 1, sl st 3, sc 10, turn. (10 sts)

**Rows 18–27:** Ch 1, sc 10, turn. (10 sts)

**Row 28:** Ch 1, in fl; sc 10, turn. (10 sts)

**Rows 29–30:** Ch 1, sc 10, turn. (10 sts)

**Row 31:** Ch 1, in bl; sc 10, turn. (10 sts)

**Rows 32–40:** Ch 1, sc 10, turn. (10 sts)

**Row 41:** Ch 4. Starting in 2nd ch from hook, sc 3, sc 10, turn. (13 sts)

**Row 42:** Ch 4. Starting in 2nd ch from hook, sc 3, sc 13, turn. (16 sts)

**Rows 43–44:** Ch 1, sc 16, turn. (16 sts)

**Row 45:** Ch 1, sl st 3, sc 13, turn. (13 sts)

**Row 46:** Ch 1, sl st 3, sc 10, turn. (10 sts)

**Rows 47–53:** Ch 1, sc 10, turn. (10 sts)

Cut yarn and fasten off, leaving a long tail for sewing.

With the surface loops of the front loader base facing out, sew row 53 to the middle of row 1.

Using 1-inch (25mm) cushion foam, cut (1) 2¾ x 6-inch (7 x 15cm) rectangle and (2) 1¼ x ¾-inch (3 x 2cm) rectangles to stuff the base and steps (or just stuff the steps with fiberfill if you prefer). Insert foam pieces between the top and bottom layers of the base. Pin or use slip rings to hold side edges tog, inserting step pieces as you pin. Sew edges together with a whip stitch.

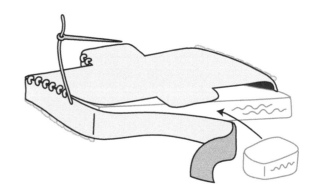

## CAB

Starting with black, loosely ch 8.

**Rnd 1:** Starting in 2nd ch and working in back ridge loops, sc 6, sc 4 in next ch. Rotate chain so front side of chain is facing up. Starting in front side of the next ch, sc 5, sc 3 in front side of next ch. (18 sts)

**Rnd 2:** Sc 3 in next st, sc 5, sc 3 in next st, sc 2, sc 3 in next st, sc 5, sc 3 in next st, sc 2. (26 sts)

**Rnd 3:** Sc 1, sc 3 in next st, sc 7, sc 3 in next st, sc 4, sc 3 in next st, sc 7, sc 3 in next st, sc 3. (34 sts)

**Rnd 4:** Sc 2, sc 3 in next st, sc 9, sc 3 in next st, sc 6, sc 3 in next st, sc 9, sc 3 in next st, sc 4. (42 sts)

**Rnd 5:** Sc 3, sc 3 in next st, sc 11, sc 3 in next st, sc 8, sc 3 in next st, sc 11, sc 3 in next st, sc 5. (50 sts)

### Cab back wall

To begin: Sl st 5, turn.

**Row 1:** Ch 1, in fl; sc 10. Pm in next st. Turn work. (10 sts)

**Rows 2–3:** Ch 1, sc 10, turn. (10 sts)

**Rows 4:** Ch 1, sc 1, cut black, leaving a 36-inch (.9m) tail to work with, change to white, sc 8, rejoin black from skein, sc 1, turn. (10 sts)

**Rows 5–8:** Ch 1, sc 1, change to white, sc 8, change to black, sc 1, turn. (10 sts)

**Row 9:** Ch 1, sc 1, change to white, sc2tog, sc 4, sc2tog, change to black, sc 1, turn. (8 sts)

**Rows 10–14:** Ch 1, sc 1, change to white, sc 6, change to black, sc 1, turn. (8 sts)

Cut white.

**Row 15:** Ch 1, sc2tog, sc 4, sc2tog, turn. (6 sts)

**Row 16:** Ch 1, sc 6, turn. (6 sts)

Cut yarn and fasten off, leaving a long tail for sewing.

### Side wall 1

**Row 1:** Starting with black, (sl st, ch 1, sc 1) in fl of pm stitch to re-attach yarn. Cont working in fl; sc 14. Pm in next st. Turn work. (15 sts)

**Rows 2–3:** Ch 1, sc 15, turn. (15 sts)

**Row 4:** Ch 1, sc 1, cut black, leaving a 36-inch (.9m) tail to work with, change to white, sc 13, rejoin black from skein, sc 1, turn. (15 sts)

**Row 5:** Ch 1, sc 1, change to white, sc 13, change to black, sc 1, turn. (15 sts)

**Row 6:** Ch 1, sc 1, change to white, sc2tog, sc 11, change to black, sc 1, turn. (14 sts)

**Rows 7–8:** Ch 1, sc 1, change to white, sc 12, change to black, sc 1, turn. (14 sts)

**Row 9:** Ch 1, sc 1, change to white, sc 10, sc2tog, change to black, sc 1, turn. (13 sts)

**Rows 10–11:** Ch 1, sc 1, change to white, sc 11, change to black, sc 1, turn. (13 sts)

**Row 12:** Ch 1, sc 1, change to white, sc2tog, sc 9 change to black, sc 1, turn. (12 sts)

**Rows 13–14:** Ch 1, sc 1, change to white, sc 10, change to black, sc 1, turn. (12 sts)

Cut white.

**Row 15:** Ch 1, sc 10, sc2tog, turn. (11 sts)

**Row 16:** Ch 1, sc 11, turn. (11 sts)

Cut yarn and fasten off, leaving a long tail for sewing.

### Front cab wall

**Row 1:** Starting with black, (sl st, ch 1, sc 1) in fl of pm stitch to re-attach yarn. Cont working in fl; sc 9. Pm in next st. Turn work. (10 sts)

Starting at row 2, rep back cab wall.

### Side wall 2

**Row 1:** Starting with black, (sl st, ch 1, sc 1) in fl of pm stitch to re-attach yarn. Cont working in fl; sc 14. Turn work. (15 sts)

**Rows 2–3:** Ch 1, sc 15, turn. (15 sts)

**Row 4:** Ch 1, sc 1, cut black leaving a 36-inch (.9m) tail to work with, change to white, sc 13, rejoin black from skein, sc 1, turn. (15 sts)

**Row 5:** Ch 1, sc 1, change to white, sc 13, change to black, sc 1, turn. (15 sts)

**Row 6:** Ch 1, sc 1, change to white, sc 11, sc2tog, change to black, sc 1, turn. (14 sts)

**Rows 7–8:** Ch 1, sc 1, change to white, sc 12, change to black, sc 1, turn. (14 sts)

**Row 9:** Ch 1, sc 1, change to white, sc2tog, sc 10, change to black, sc 1, turn. (13 sts)

**Rows 10–11:** Ch 1, sc 1, change to white, sc 11, change to black, sc 1, turn. (13 sts)

**Row 12:** Ch 1, sc 1, change to white, sc 9, sc2tog, change to black, sc 1, turn. (12 sts)

# FRONT LOADER ////

**Rows 13–14:** Ch 1, sc 1, change to white, sc 10, change to black, sc 1, turn. (12 sts)

Cut white.

**Row 15:** Ch 1, sc2tog, sc 10, turn. (11 sts)

**Row 16:** Ch 1, sc 11, turn. (11 sts)

Cut yarn and fasten off, leaving a long tail for sewing.

Sew up side edges.

## CAB ROOF

In yellow, loosely ch 6.

**Rnd 1:** Starting in 2nd ch and working in back ridge loops, sc 4, sc 4 in next ch. Rotate chain so front side of chain is facing up. Starting in front side of the next ch, sc 3, sc 3 in front side of next ch. (14 sts)

**Rnd 2:** Sc 3 in next st, sc 3, sc 3 in next st, sc 2, sc 3 in next st, sc 3, sc 3 in next st, sc 2. (22 sts)

**Rnd 3:** Sc 1, sc 3 in next st, sc 5, sc 3 in next st, sc 4, sc 3 in next st, sc 5, sc 3 in next st, sc 3. (30 sts)

**Rnd 4:** Sc 2, sc 3 in next st, sc 7, sc 3 in next st, sc 6, sc 3 in next st, sc 7, sc 3 in next st, sc 4. (38 sts)

**Rnd 5:** Sc 3, sc 3 in next st, sc 9, sc 3 in next st, sc 8, sc 3 in next st, sc 9, sc 3 in next st, sc 5. (46 sts)

**Rnd 6:** In bl; sc 46. (46 sts)

**Rnd 7:** In bl; sc 3, sc3tog, sc 9, sc3tog, sc 8, sc3tog, sc 9, sc3tog, sc 5. (38 sts)

**Rnd 8:** Sc 2, sc3tog, sc 7, sc3tog, sc 6, sc3tog, sc 7, sc3tog, sc 4. (30 sts)

**Rnd 9:** Sc 1, sc3tog, sc 5, sc3tog, sc 4, sc3tog, sc 5, sc3tog, sc 3. (22 sts)

Using foam stabilizer, cut out (1) 3¼ x 3-inch (8 x 8cm) rectangle. Insert foam into roof.

**Rnd 10:** Sc3tog, sc 3, sc3tog, sc 2, sc3tog, sc 3, sc3tog, sc 2. (14 sts)

**Rnd 11:** Sc 14. (14 sts)

Cut yarn and fasten off, leaving a long tail for sewing.

Sew the roof seam closed. With roof seam

side down, sew bottom edge of roof to the open edge of the cab. Add more stuffing if needed before closing seam.

## CAB HOOD

Starting with yellow, loosely ch 8.

**Rnd 1:** Starting in 2nd ch and working in back ridge loops, sc 6, sc 4 in next ch. Rotate chain so front side of chain is facing up. Starting in front side of the next ch, sc 5, sc 3 in front side of next ch. (18 sts)

**Rnd 2:** Sc 3 in next st, sc 5, sc 3 in next st, sc 2, sc 3 in next st, sc 5, sc 3 in next st, sc 2. (26 sts)

**Rnd 3:** Sc 2 in next st, sc 3 in next st, sc 7, sc 3 in next st, sc 4, sc 3 in next st, sc 7, sc 3 in next st, sc 2 in next st, sc 2. (36 sts)

**Rnd 4:** Sc 3, sc 3 in next st, sc 9 sc 3 in next st, sc2tog, sc 2, sc2tog, sc 3 in next st, sc 9, sc 3 in next st, sc 5. (42 sts)

### Hood back wall

To begin: Sl st 4, turn.

**Row 1:** Ch 1, in fl; sc 10. Pm in next st. Turn work. (10 sts)

**Rows 2–6:** Ch 1, sc 10, turn. (10 sts)

**Row 7:** Ch 1, sc 10. (10 sts)

Cut yarn and fasten off, leaving a long tail for sewing.

### Hood side wall 1

**Row 1:** With yellow, (sl st, ch 1, sc 1) in fl of pm stitch to re-attach yarn. Cont working in fl; sc 11. Pm in next st. Turn work. (12 sts)

**Rows 2–3:** Ch 1, sc 12, turn. (12 sts)

**Row 4:** Ch 1, sc2tog, sc 10, turn. (11 sts)

**Row 5:** Ch 1, sc 11, turn. (11 sts)

**Row 6:** Ch 1, sc2tog, sc 9, turn. (10 sts)

**Row 7:** Ch 1, sc 5, sl st 5. (10 sts)

Cut yarn and fasten off, leaving a long tail for sewing.

### Hood front

**Row 1:** Starting with yellow, (sl st, ch 1, sc 1) in fl of pm stitch to re-attach yarn. Cont working in fl; sc 7. Pm in next st. Turn work. (8 sts)

**Rows 2–3:** Ch 1, sc 8, turn. (8 sts)

**Row 4:** Ch 1, sc2tog, sc 4, sc2tog, turn. (6 sts)

**Row 5:** Ch 1, sc 6, turn. (6 sts)

**Row 6:** Ch 1, sc 2, sc2tog, sc 2, turn. (5 sts)

Change to black.

**Rows 7–10:** Ch 1, sc 5, turn. (5 sts)

**Row 11:** Ch 1, sc 2, sc 2 in next st, sc 2, turn. (6 sts)

**Rows 12–13:** Ch 1, sc 6, turn. (6 sts)

**Row 14:** Ch 1, sc 2 in next st, sc 4, sc 2 in next st. (8 sts)

**Rows 15–16:** Ch 1, sc 8, turn. (8 sts)

**Row 17:** Ch 1, sc 2 in next st, sc 6, sc 2 in next st. (10 sts)

Cut yarn and fasten off, leaving a long tail for sewing.

**Hood side wall 2**
**Row 1:** With yellow, (sl st, ch 1, sc 1) in fl of pm stitch to re-attach yarn. Cont working in fl; sc 11. Turn work. (12 sts)

**Rows 2–3:** Ch 1, sc 12, turn. (12 sts)

**Row 4:** Ch 1, sc 10, sc2tog, turn. (11 sts)

**Row 5:** Ch 1, sc 11, turn. (11 sts)

**Row 6:** Ch 1, sc 9, sc2tog, turn. (10 sts)

**Row 7:** Ch 1, sl st 5, sc 5. (5 sts)

Cut yarn and fasten off, leaving a long tail for sewing.

Sew edges together with a whip stitch and stuff before closing seam.

## GRILL

Using dark gray, loosely ch 9.

**Row 1:** Starting in 2nd chain from hook, sc 8, turn. (8 sts)

**Row 2:** Ch 1, sl st 8 loosely, turn. (8 sts)

**Row 3:** Ch 1, sc 8, turn. (8 sts)

**Row 4:** Ch 1, sl st 8 loosely, turn. (8 sts)

**Row 5:** Ch 1, sc2tog, sc 4, sc2tog, turn. (6 sts)

**Row 6:** Ch 1, sl st 6 loosely, turn. (6 sts)

**Row 7:** Ch 1, sc 2, sc2tog, sc 2, turn. (5 sts)

**Row 8:** Ch 1, sl st 5 loosely, turn. (5 sts)

# FRONT LOADER ////

Sl st around outside edges of the grill until you have reached the other side of row 8.

Cut yarn and fasten off, leaving a long tail for sewing.

Sew the grill onto the front of the hood.

Line up the bottom of the pieces and sew the back hood wall to the front of the cab. Sew the cab and hood to the front loader base (the larger end of the base will be under the cab part of the backhoe). The cab and hood will overhang the base slightly on either end.

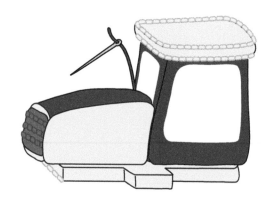

Double up black yarn on a tapestry needle and embroider a chain stitch around each window and add some window pane details (refer to photos for reference).

## SMOKESTACK

With dark gray, make a 4-st adjustable ring.

**Rnd 1:** In bl; sc 4. (4 sts)

**Rnds 2–4:** Sc 4. (4 sts)

**Smokestack flap**
In fl of next st, (sl st 1, ch 2, hdc 2, ch 2, sl st 1). Cut yarn and fasten off.

Sew bottom of smokestack to top of hood.

## FRONT TIRE (MAKE 2)

Using black, make a 6-st adjustable ring.

**Rnd 1:** Sc 2 in each st around. (12 sts)

**Rnd 2:** *Sc 1, sc 2 in next st; rep from * 5 more times. (18 sts)

**Rnd 3:** *Sc 2, sc 2 in next st; rep from * 5 more times. (24 sts)

**Rnds 4–5:** Sc 24. (24 sts)

**Rnd 6:** *Sc 2, sc2tog; rep from * 5 more times. (18 sts)

**Rnd 7:** *Sc 1, sc2tog; rep from * 5 more times. (12 sts)

Stuff wheel.

**Rnd 8:** Sc2tog 6 times. (6 sts)

Cut yarn and fasten off, leaving a long tail for sewing. Close the 6-st hole.

Thread the yarn tail back and forth through the center of the tire 3 to 4 times, pulling tightly as you sew to shape the tire.

## FRONT TIRE HUBCAP (MAKE 2)

Using light gray, make a 4-st adjustable ring.

**Rnd 1:** Sc 2 in each st around. (8 sts)

Cut yarn and fasten off, leaving a long tail for sewing.

Sew the hubcaps to the sides of the tires.

## BACK TIRE (MAKE 2)

Using black, make a 6-st adjustable ring.

**Rnd 1:** Sc 2 in each st around. (12 sts)

**Rnd 2:** *Sc 1, sc 2 in next st; rep from * 5 more times. (18 sts)

**Rnd 3:** *Sc 2, sc 2 in next st; from * 5 more times. (24 sts)

**Rnd 4:** *Sc 3, sc 2 in next st; rep from * 5 more times. (30 sts)

**Rnd 5:** *Sc 4, sc 2 in next st; rep from * 5 more times. (36 sts)

**Rnds 6–7:** Sc 36. (36 sts)

**Rnd 8:** *Sc 4, sc2tog; rep from * 5 more times. (30 sts)

**Rnd 9:** *Sc 3, sc2tog; rep from * 5 more times. (24 sts)

**Rnd 10:** *Sc 2, sc2tog; rep from * 5 more times. (18 sts)

**Rnd 11:** *Sc 1, sc2tog; rep from * 5 more times. (12 sts)

Stuff wheel.

**Rnd 12:** Sc2tog 6 times. (6 sts)

Fasten off yarn, leaving a long tail for sewing. Close the 6-st hole.

Thread the yarn tail back and forth through the center of the tire 3 to 4 times, pulling tightly as you sew to shape the tire.

## BACK TIRE HUBCAP (MAKE 2)

Using light gray, make a 6-st adjustable ring.

**Rnd 1:** Sc 2 in each st around. (12 sts)

**Rnd 2:** *Sc 1, sc 2 in next st; rep from * around. (18 sts)

Cut yarn and fasten off, leaving a long tail for sewing.

Sew the hubcaps to the sides of the tires.

## BACK TIRE FENDER (MAKE 2)

Using dark gray make a 6-st adjustable ring.

**Rnd 1:** Sc 2 in each st around. (12 sts)

**Rnds 2–18:** Sc 12. (12 sts)

**Rnd 19:** Sc2tog 6 times. (6 sts)

Fasten off yarn, leaving a long tail for sewing.

Wrap fenders over the top of the large tires and sew in place.

Sew the smaller front tires of the sides of the front loader base in front of the steps. Sew the larger back tires with fenders to the back of the front loader base.

## AXLE PIN (MAKE 4)

In dark gray, make a 6-st adjustable ring.

**Rnd 1:** In bl; sc 6. (6 sts)

**Rnd 2:** Sc2tog 3 times. (3 sts)

Cut yarn and fasten off, leaving a long tail for sewing.

Cinch hole closed with yarn tail. Thread the yarn tail back and forth through the center of the axle pin 3 to 4 times, pulling tightly as you sew to flatten the axle pin.

**TIP:** For vehicles intended for children 3 years and older, you can also use ½–¾-inch (13–19mm) shank buttons for axle pins.

# FRONT LOADER ////

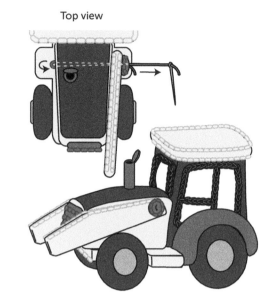

Top view

## LOADER BOOM ARM (MAKE 2)

With yellow, loosely ch 16.

**Row 1:** Starting in 2nd ch from hook, sc 15, turn. (15 sts)

**Row 2:** Ch 1, sc 2, hdc 3, dc 2, hdc 2, sc 6, turn. (15 sts)

**Row 3:** Ch 1, sc 6, hdc 2, dc 2, hdc 2, sc 3, turn. (15 sts)

**Row 4:** Ch 1, in fl; sc 15, turn. (15 sts)

**Row 5:** Ch 1, in bl; sc 6, hdc 2, dc 2, hdc 2, sc 3, turn. (15 sts)

**Row 6:** Ch 1, sc 2, hdc 3, dc 2, hdc 2, sc 6, turn. (15 sts)

**Row 7:** Ch 1, sc 15, turn. (15 sts)

**Row 8:** Ch 1, in fl; sc 15, turn. (15 sts)

Cut yarn and fasten off, leaving a long tail for sewing.

Using foam stabilizer, cut (2) loader boom arm pieces from template (page 112). With surface loops of rows 4–5 facing out, insert foam pieces and close seams.

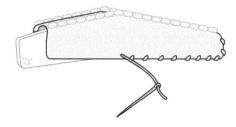

With the hdc/dc shaping pointed up, place the loader boom arms on either side of the cab hood. The thinner end of each loader boom is closest to the windshield.

Thread the axle pin tail through the loader boom arm and through the hood to create a pivot point. Secure yarn to the opposite side of the hood, then thread the yarn back to the axle pin, taking care to go through the same holes. Rep on the other loader boom arm.

## LOADER BUCKET SIDE (MAKE 2)

With light gray, make an 8-st adjustable ring.

**Rnd 1:** Sc 2 in each st around. (16 sts)

**Rnd 2:** *Sc 1, sc 2 in next st; rep from * around. (24 sts)

**Rnd 3:** *Sc 2, sc 2 in next st; rep from * around. (32 sts)

**Rnd 4:** *Sc 3, sc 2 in next st; rep from * around. (40 sts)

**Rnd 5:** In bl; sc 20 (leave remaining 20 sts unworked) Cut yarn and fasten off, leaving a long tail for sewing.

Using foam stabilizer, cut out (1) 3-inch (8cm) circle. Cut circle in half. Fold loader bucket side in half so the sc 20 from rnd 5 is on one half. Insert (1) foam semi-circle and sew seams shut. Rep on other side.

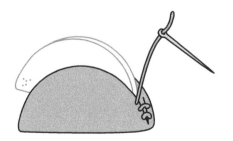

## LOADER BUCKET CENTER

With light gray, loosely ch 16.

**Row 1:** Starting in 2nd ch from hook, sc 15, turn. (15 sts)

**Rows 2–20:** Ch 1, sc 15, turn. (15 sts)

**Row 21:** Ch 1, in bl; sc 15, turn. (15 sts)

**Row 22:** Ch 1, in fl; sc 15, turn. (15 sts)

**Rows 23–40:** Ch 1, sc 15, turn. (15 sts)

**Row 41:** Fold piece in half and line up row 1 and row 40 with the surface loops of rows 21 and 22 facing out. Holding edges together, sc 15 with row 1 and row 40 tog, turn. (15 sts)

### Bucket teeth

**Row 42:** *Sl st 1, (sl st 1, ch 2, hdc 2, ch 2, sl st 1) in next st, sl st 1; rep from * to end.

Cut yarn and fasten off, leaving a long tail for sewing.

Using foam stabilizer, cut out (1) 4 x 5-inch (10 x 13cm) rectangle and insert between the loader bucket center layers. Sew up side seams with a whip stitch.

Match up and pin the whip-stitched sides of the loader bucket center with the rounded sides of the loader bucket sides. Sew the edges of the loader bucket center to the inside surfaces of the loader bucket sides.

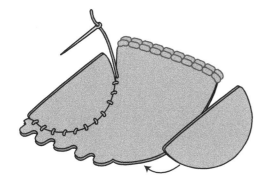

## LOADER BUCKET AXLE

With dark gray, make a 5-st adjustable ring.

**Rnd 1:** In bl; sc 5. (5 sts)

**Rnds 2–12:** Sc 5, stuffing the axle as you work.

**Rnd 13:** In bl; sc 5. (5 sts)

Stuff loader bucket axle. Cut yarn, fasten off, and close hole, leaving a long tail for sewing.

**TIP:** Use the back of a pencil, a chopstick, or the handle of a smaller crochet hook to help stuff the axle.

Using leftover yarn tail, attach loader bucket axle to back of loader bucket, leaving 4 rows of space between the loader bucket axle and the top of the loader bucket.

Position the ends of the loader boom arms next to the sides of the loader bucket axle. Draw the axle pin yarn tail through the side of one loader boom arm and into the side of the loader boom axle. Secure yarn to the side of the loader boom axle, then thread the yarn back to front of the axle pin, taking care to go through the same holes to maintain the pivot point. Rep 1 to 2 more times before securing yarn and weaving in end. Rep on other loader boom arm.

Top view

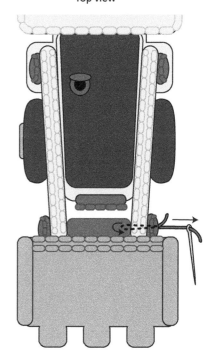

Weave in any remaining yarn tails.

# BACKHOE

**FINISHED SIZE:** 25 (with buckets extended) x 7 x 7 in. (64 x 18 x 18cm) /// **YARN WEIGHT:**

Wen your job requires a bucket on both ends, look no further than Backhoe to get the work done! Starting with the front loader pattern (page 34), this project includes a working excavator arm and removable bucket. For some additional fun, you can also add the auger attachment from the excavator pattern on page 80.

## MATERIALS & TOOLS

- Bulky-weight yarn in black (100 yds/91m), dark gray (150 yds/137m), light gray (150 yds/137m), white (100 yds/91m), and yellow (300 yds/274m)
- Hook size I (5.5mm)
- Place marker
- Scissors
- Tapestry needle
- Polyester fiberfill
- 1-in. (25mm)-thick cushion foam
- Foam stabilizer

## INSTRUCTIONS

### TRUCK

Make the Front Loader (page 34) as instructed.

### AXLE PIN (MAKE 6)

In dark gray, make a 6-st adjustable ring.

**Rnd 1:** In bl; sc 6. (6 sts)

**Rnd 2:** Sc2tog 3 times. (3 sts)

Cut yarn and fasten off, leaving a long tail for sewing.

Cinch hole closed with yarn tail. Thread the yarn tail back and forth through the center of the axle pin 3 to 4 times, pulling tightly as you sew to flatten the axle pin.

## BOOM BRACKET

In yellow, loosely ch 13.

**Rnd 1:** Starting in 2nd ch and working in back ridge loops, sc 11, sc 4 in next ch. Rotate chain so front side of chain is facing up. Starting in front side of the next ch, sc 10, sc 3 in front side of next ch. (28 sts)

**Rnd 2:** Sc 3 in next st, sc 10, sc 3 in next st, sc 2, sc 3 in next st, sc 10, sc 3 in next st, sc 2. (36 sts)

**Rnd 3:** In bl; sc 36. (36 sts)

**Rnd 4:** In bl; sc3tog, sc 10, sc3tog, sc 2, sc3tog, sc 10, sc3tog, sc 2. (28 sts)

Cut yarn and fasten off, leaving a long tail for sewing.

Using foam stabilizer, cut out (1) 1 x 3½-inch ( 2.5 x 9 cm) rectangle. With a pen, draw a vertical line at 1¼ inches (3cm) and 2¼ inches (6cm) onto

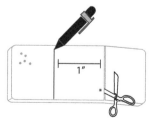

*Cut top layer of foam only

the rectangle. With scissors or a straight edge, carefully score just one side of the foam to create three sections. Insert into boom bracket, scored side first into the seam opening. Sew seam closed in a straight line using a mattress stitch.

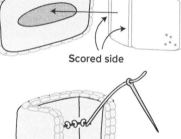

Scored side

Fold the boom bracket toward the sewn seam at the points where the foam is scored. Sew just the top and bottom of the 1-inch (25mm) middle section to the back of the front loader base with the boom bracket's seam side facing out.

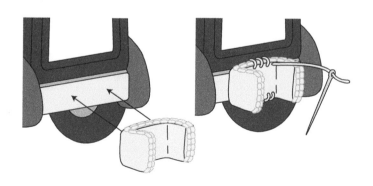

## BOOM

In yellow, loosely ch 16.

**Rnd 1:** Starting in 2nd ch and working in back ridge loops, sc 14, sc 4 in next ch. Rotate chain so front side of chain is facing up. Starting in front side of the next ch, sc 13, sc 2 in front side of next ch. (33 sts)

**Rnd 2:** Sc 2 in next st, sc 7, hdc 6, dc 2 in next 4 sts, hdc 6, sc 7, sc 2 in next 2 sts. (40 sts)

**Rnd 3:** Bpsc 40. (40 sts)

**Rnds 4–5:** Sc 40. (40 sts)

**Rnd 6:** Bpsc 40. (40 sts)

**Rnd 7:** Sc 40. (40 sts)

**Rnd 8:** Sc2tog, sc 7, hdc 6, dc2tog 4 times, hdc 6, sc 7, sc2tog 2 times. (33 sts)

Cut yarn and fasten off, leaving a long tail for sewing.

### Boom tab (make 2)

The top of the boom is the thinner/tapered end. At the top of the boom on one side, locate the center surface stitch from rnd 3. Mark this stitch with a pm. Count 3 sts to the right of this st and pm. Remove the center pm.

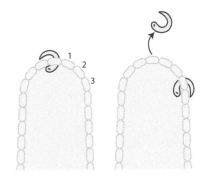

**Row 1:** With yellow, begin by working in the pm surface stitch, (sl st, ch 1, sc 1). Cont working into the next 6 sts; hdc 1, dc 3, hdc 1, sc 1, sl st 1, turn.

**Row 2:** Sk sl st, sc 2, sc 2 in next 3 sts, sc 2, turn. (10 sts)

**Row 3:** Ch 1, in bl; sc 10, turn. (10 sts)

**Row 4:** Ch 1, in fl; sc 2, sc2tog 3 times, sc 2. Cut yarn and fasten off, leaving a long tail for sewing. (7 sts)

Rep on other side of boom.

Using 1-inch (25mm) cushion foam, cut (1) boom piece from template (page 112). Insert foam inside boom. Close up the seam in a straight line using a mattress stitch.

Using foam stabilizer, cut (2) boom tab pieces from template (page 113). Insert into the boom tab spaces and sew seams down to the top of the boom.

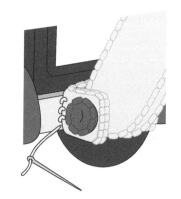

Position the larger bottom end of boom between the sides of the folded boom bracket. Draw the yarn tail of 1 axle pin through one side of the boom bracket, through the boom, and

through the opposite side of the bracket. Pull firmly and fasten off. Starting on the opposite side, draw the yarn tail of a 2nd axle pin through the all the same openings as the first axle pin. Secure yarn under the first axle pin, pulling firmly to create a tight pivot.

Once boom is attached to boom bracket, feel free to add a few more stitches in yellow along the sides of the center section of the boom bracket for additional support.

## EXCAVATOR BUCKET ARM

In yellow, loosely ch 11.

**Rnd 1:** Starting in 2nd ch and working in back ridge loops, sc 9, sc 3 in next ch. Rotate chain so front side of chain is facing up. Starting in front side of the next ch, sc 8, sc 2 in front side of next ch. (22 sts)

**Rnd 2:** Sc 2 in next st, sc 8, sc 2 in next 3 sts, sc 8, sc 2 in next 2 sts. (28 sts)

**Rnds 3–4:** Bpsc 28. (28 sts)

**Rnd 5:** Sc2tog, sc 8, sc2tog 3 times, sc 8, sc2tog 2 times. (22 sts)

Cut yarn and fasten off, leaving a long tail for sewing.

Using 1-inch (25mm) cushion foam, cut (1) excavator bucket arm from template (page 112). Place foam inside excavator bucket arm and sew seam closed in a straight line using a mattress stitch.

Place one end of the excavator bucket arm between the two boom tabs at the top of the boom. Draw the yarn tail of 1 axle pin through one side of the first boom tab, through the excavator arm, and through the opposite side of the 2nd boom tab. Pull firmly and fasten off. Starting on the opposite side of the 2nd boom tab, draw the yarn tail of the 2nd axle pin through all the same openings as the first axle pin. Secure yarn under the first axle pin, pulling firmly to create a tight pivot.

## EXCAVATOR BUCKET SIDE (MAKE 2)

With light gray, make an 8-st adjustable ring.

**Rnd 1:** Sc 2 in each st around. (16 sts)

**Rnd 2:** *Sc 1, sc 2 in next st; rep from * around. (24 sts)

**Rnd 3:** *Sc 2, sc 2 in next st; rep from * around. (32 sts)

**Rnd 4:** In bl; sc 16 (leave remaining 16 sts unworked). (16 sts)

Cut yarn and fasten off, leaving a long tail for sewing.

Using foam stabilizer, cut out (1) 2¼-inch (6cm) circle. Cut circle in half. Fold excavator bucket side in half so sc 16 from rnd 4 is on one half. Insert 1 foam semi-circle and sew seams shut. Rep on other side.

## EXCAVATOR BUCKET CENTER

With light gray, loosely ch 10.

**Row 1:** Starting in 2nd ch from hook, sc 9, turn. (9 sts)

**Rows 2–14:** Ch 1, sc 9, turn. (9 sts)

**Row 15:** Ch 1, in bl; sc 9, turn. (9 sts)

**Row 16:** Ch 1, in fl; sc 9, turn. (9 sts)

**Rows 17–28:** Ch 1, sc 9, turn. (9 sts)

**Row 29:** Fold piece in half and line up row 1 and row 28 with the surface loops of rows 15 and 16 facing out. Holding edges together, sc 9 with row 1 and row 28 tog, turn. (9 sts)

**Row 30:** *Sl st 1, (sl st 1, ch 2, hdc 2, ch 2, sl st 1) in next st, sl st 1; rep from * to end.

Cut yarn and fasten off, leaving a long tail for sewing.

Using foam stabilizer, cut out (1) 2½ x 3¾-inch (6 x 10cm) rectangle and insert between the excavator bucket center layers. Sew up side seams with a whip stitch.

Match up the whip-stitched sides of the excavator bucket center with the rounded sides of the excavator bucket sides. Sew the edges of the excavator bucket center to the inside surface of the excavator bucket sides.

## EXCAVATOR BUCKET STRAP (MAKE 2)

In light gray, loosely ch 7.

Cut yarn and fasten off, leaving a long tail for sewing.

Attach the ends of the straps to the top edge of the excavator bucket to the left and right of center with about 1 st of space between them to make two loops. Attach the last two axle pins to the end of the excavator bucket arm and slide the bucket loops over the pins to attach the bucket. It should be a snug fit.

Weave in any remaining yarn tails.

# STEAMROLLER

**FINISHED SIZE:** 10½ x 7 x 6½ in. (27 x 18 x 17cm)  /// **YARN WEIGHT:**

**W**hen smooth and flat is the name of the game, you can't beat this chunky steamroller with an oversized spinning front roller. Perfect for road repair, foundation work, and asphalt smoothing, Steamroller loves to keep things rolling.

## MATERIALS & TOOLS

- Bulky-weight yarn in black (100 yds/91m), dark gray (150 yds/137m), light gray (150 yds/137m), red (25 yds/23m), white (100 yds/91m), and yellow (300 yds/274m)
- Hook size I (5.5mm)
- Stitch marker
- Scissors
- Tapestry needle
- Sewing needle and thread
- Polyester fiberfill
- 1-in. (25mm)-thick cushion foam
- Foam stabilizer

## INSTRUCTIONS

### CAB

Starting with yellow, loosely ch 6.

**Rnd 1:** Starting in 2nd ch and working in back ridge loops, sc 4, sc 4 in next ch. Rotate chain so front side of chain is facing up. Starting in front side of the next ch, sc 3, sc 3 in front side of next ch. (14 sts)

**Rnd 2:** Sc 3 in next st, sc 3, sc 3 in next st, sc 2, sc 3 in next st, sc 3, sc 3 in next st, sc 2. (22 sts)

**Rnd 3:** Sc 1, sc 3 in next st, sc 5, sc 3 in next st, sc 4, sc 3 in next st, sc 5, sc 3 in next st, sc 3. (30 sts)

**Rnd 4:** Sc 2, sc 3 in next st, sc 7 3 in next st, sc 6, sc 3 in next st, sc 7, sc 3 in next st, sc 4. (38 sts)

# STEAMROLLER ////

**Rnd 5:** Sc 3, sc 3 in next st, sc 9, sc 3 in next st, sc 8, sc 3 in next st, sc 9, sc 3 in next st, sc 5. (46 sts)

## Cab back wall

To begin: Sl st 5, turn.

**Row 1:** Ch 1, in fl; sc 10. Pm in next st. Turn work. (10 sts)

**Rows 2–8:** Ch 1, sc 10, turn. (10 sts)

Cut yellow, change to black. Keep yarn tails on front side of work for row 9.

**Row 9:** Ch 1, sc 1, cut black, leaving a 48-inch (1.2m) tail to work with, change to white, sc2tog, sc 4, sc2tog, rejoin black from skein, sc 1, turn. (8 sts)

**Rows 10–14:** Ch 1, sc 1, change to white, sc 6, change to black, sc 1, turn. (8 sts)

Cut white.

**Row 15:** Ch 1, sc2tog, sc 4, sc2tog, turn. (6 sts)

**Row 16:** Ch 1, sc 6, turn. (6 sts)

Cut yarn and fasten off, leaving a long tail for sewing.

## Side wall 1

**Row 1:** Starting with yellow, (sl st, ch 1, sc 1) in fl of pm stitch to re-attach yarn. Cont working in fl; sc 12. Pm in next st. Turn work. (13 sts)

**Rows 2–3:** Ch 1, sc 13, turn. (13 sts)

Cut yellow. Change to black. Keep yarn tails on the back side of your work for row 4.

**Row 4:** Ch 1, sc 1, cut black, leaving a 48-inch (1.2m) tail to work with, change to white, sc 11, rejoin black from skein, sc 1, turn. (13 sts)

**Row 5:** Ch 1, sc 1, change to white, sc 11, change to black, sc 1, turn. (13 sts)

**Row 6:** Ch 1, sc 1, change to white, sc2tog, sc 9, change to black, sc 1, turn. (12 sts)

**Rows 7–8:** Ch 1, sc 1, change to white, sc 10, change to black, sc 1, turn. (12 sts)

**Row 9:** Ch 1, sc 1, change to white, sc 8, sc2tog, change to black, sc 1, turn. (11 sts)

**Rows 10–11:** Ch 1, sc 1, change to white, sc 9, change to black, sc 1, turn. (11 sts)

**Row 12:** Ch 1, sc 1, change to white, sc2tog, sc 7 change to black, sc 1, turn. (10 sts)

**Rows 13–14:** Ch 1, sc 1, change to white, sc 8, change to black, sc 1, turn. (10 sts)

Cut white.

**Row 15:** Ch 1, sc 8, sc2tog, turn. (9 sts)

**Row 16:** Ch 1, sc 9, turn. (9 sts)

Cut yarn and fasten off, leaving a long tail for sewing.

## Front cab wall

**Row 1:** Starting with yellow, (sl st, ch 1, sc 1) in fl of pm stitch to re-attach yarn. Cont working in fl; sc 9. Pm in next st. Turn work. (10 sts)

Rep cab back wall starting at row 2.

## Side wall 2

**Row 1:** Starting with yellow, (sl st, ch 1, sc 1) in fl of pm stitch to re-attach yarn. Cont working in fl; sc 12. Turn work. (13 sts)

**Rows 2–3:** Ch 1, sc 13, turn. (13 sts)

Cut yellow. Change to black. Keep yarn tails at the back side of work for row 4.

**Row 4:** Ch 1, sc 1, cut black, leaving a 48-inch (1.2m) tail to work with, change to white, sc 11, rejoin black from skein, sc 1, turn. (13 sts)

**Row 5:** Ch 1, sc 1, change to white, sc 11, change to black, sc 1, turn. (13 sts)

**Row 6:** Ch 1, sc 1, change to white, sc 9, sc2tog, change to black, sc 1, turn. (12 sts)

**Rows 7–8:** Ch 1, sc 1, change to white, sc 10, change to black, sc 1, turn. (12 sts)

**Row 9:** Ch 1, sc 1, change to white, sc2tog, sc 8, change to black, sc 1, turn. (11 sts)

**Rows 10–11:** Ch 1, sc 1, change to white, sc 9, change to black, sc 1, turn. (11 sts)

**Row 12:** Ch 1, sc 1, change to white, sc 7, sc2tog, change to black, sc 1, turn. (10 sts)

**Rows 13–14:** Ch 1, sc 1, change to white, sc 8, change to black, sc 1, turn. (10 sts)

Cut white.

**Row 15:** Ch 1, sc2tog, sc 8, turn. (9 sts)

**Row 16:** Ch 1, sc 9, turn. (9 sts)

Cut yarn and fasten off, leaving a long tail for sewing.

Sew up side edges.

## CAB ROOF

In yellow, loosely ch 6.

**Rnd 1:** Starting in 2nd ch and working in back ridge loops, sc 4, sc 4 in next ch. Rotate chain so front side of chain is facing up. Starting in front side of the next ch, sc 3, sc 3 in front side of next ch. (14 sts)

# STEAMROLLER ////

**Rnd 2:** Sc 3 in next st, sc 3, sc 3 in next st, sc 2, sc 3 in next st, sc 3, sc 3 in next st, sc 2. (22 sts)

**Rnd 3:** Sc 1, sc 3 in next st, sc 5, sc 3 in next st, sc 4, sc 3 in next st, sc 5, sc 3 in next st, sc 3. (30 sts)

**Rnd 4:** Sc 2, sc 3 in next st, sc 7, sc 3 in next st, sc 6, sc 3 in next st, sc 7, sc 3 in next st, sc 4. (38 sts)

**Rnd 5:** Sc 3, sc 3 in next st, sc 9, sc 3 in next st, sc 8, sc 3 in next st, sc 9, sc 3 in next st, sc 5. (46 sts)

**Rnd 6:** In bl; sc 46. (46 sts)

**Rnd 7:** In bl; sc 3, sc3tog, sc 9, sc3tog, sc 8, sc3tog, sc 9, sc3tog, sc 5. (38 sts)

**Rnd 8:** Sc 2, sc3tog, sc 7, sc3tog, sc 6, sc3tog, sc 7, sc3tog, sc 4. (30 sts)

**Rnd 9:** Sc 1, sc3tog, sc 5, sc3tog, sc 4, sc3tog, sc 5, sc3tog, sc 3. (22 sts)

Using foam stabilizer, cut out (1) 3¼ x 3-inch (8 x 8cm) rectangle. Insert foam into roof. Do not add additional stuffing.

**Rnd 10:** Sc3tog, sc 3, sc3tog, sc 2, sc3tog, sc 3, sc3tog, sc 2. (14 sts)

**Rnd 11:** Sc 14.

Cut yarn and fasten off, leaving a long tail for sewing.

Sew the roof seam closed. With roof seam side down, sew bottom edge of roof to the open edge of the cab. Add more stuffing if needed before closing seam.

## REAR ENGINE

In yellow, loosely ch 23.

**Row 1:** Starting in 2nd ch from hook and working in back ridge loops, sc 22, turn. (22 sts)

**Rows 2–8:** Ch 1, sc 22, turn.

Cut yarn and fasten off, leaving a long tail for sewing.

**Row 9:** Count 7 sts in from end. Working in fl of 7th st (sl st 1, ch 1, sc 1). Cont to work down the row in fl; sc 9 and leave remaining sts unworked. Turn. (10 sts)

**Rows 10–14:** Ch 1, sc 10, turn. (10 sts)

Cut yarn and fasten off, leaving a long tail for sewing.

With surface loops of row 9 facing out, wrap the sides of rows 1–8 around to match up with the side edges of rows 9–14. Sew the matching edges together. Sew row 14 of the rear engine to row 8 of the back cab wall. Sew the side edges of rear engine to the side edges of the back cab wall, leaving the bottom open for stuffing.

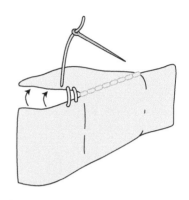

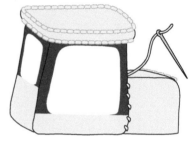

## CAB BASE

Using dark gray, loosely ch 51.

**Row 1:** Starting in 2nd ch from hook, sc 50, turn. (50 sts)

**Rows 2–3:** Ch 1, sc 50, turn. (50 sts)

Cut yarn and fasten off, leaving a long tail for sewing. Turn work.

**Row 4:** Count 21 sts in from end. Working in fl of 21 st (sl st 1, ch 1, sc 1). Cont to work down the row in fl; sc 9 and leave remaining sts unworked. Turn. (10 sts)

**Rows 5–24:** Ch 1, sc 10, turn. (10 sts)

**Row 25:** Ch 1, in bl; sc 10, turn. (10 sts)

**Rows 26–27:** Ch 1, sc 10, turn. (10 sts)

**Row 28:** Ch 1, in fl; sc 10, turn. (10 sts)

**Rows 29–48:** Ch 1, sc 10, turn. (10 sts)

Cut yarn and fasten off, leaving a long tail for sewing.

With the surface loops of the cab base facing out, sew row 48 to the middle of row 1.

Using 1-inch (25mm)-thick cushion foam, cut out (1) 6 x 2¾-inch (15 x 7cm) rectangle. Insert foam between the top and bottom layers of the cab base. Pin side edges in place and sew together with a whip stitch.

Sew the bottom of the cab and open edge of the rear engine to the top of the cab base. Stuff rear engine before closing seam.

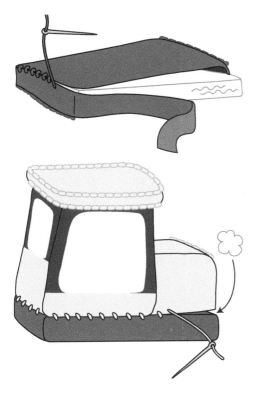

## GRILL

Using light gray, loosely ch 9.

**Row 1:** Starting in 2nd chain from hook, sc 8, turn. (8 sts)

**Row 2:** Ch 1, sl st 8 loosely, turn. (8 sts)

**Row 3:** Ch 1, sc 8, turn. (8 sts)

**Rows 4–5:** Rep rows 2–3 1 more time.

**Row 6:** Ch 1, sl st 8. (8 sts)

Cont to sl st around outside edges of the grill until you have reached the other side of row 6.

Cut yarn and fasten off, leaving a long tail for sewing.

Sew grill to middle of the yellow section at the front of cab.

Double up black yarn on a tapestry needle and embroider a chain stitch around each window as well as some window pane details (refer to photos for reference).

## SMOKESTACK

With dark gray, make a 4-st adjustable ring.

**Rnd 1:** In bl; sc 4. (4 sts)

**Rnds 2–4:** Sc 4. (4 sts)

### Smokestack flap

In fl of next st, (sl st 1, ch 2, hdc 2, ch 2, sl st 1). Cut yarn and fasten off, leaving a long tail for sewing.

Sew bottom of smokestack to top of rear engine.

# STEAMROLLER ////

## HEADLIGHT/TAIL LIGHT (MAKE 2 IN WHITE AND 2 IN RED)

Starting with red or white, make a 3-st adjustable ring.

**Rnd 1:** Sc 2 in each st around. (6 sts)

Change to dark gray.

**Rnd 2:** Sl st 6.

Cut yarn and fasten off, leaving a long tail for sewing.

Sew the two white headlights to the front of the cab near the upper corners of the grill. Sew the two red tail lights to the back corners of the rear cab.

## TIRE (MAKE 2)

Using black, make a 6-st adjustable ring.

**Rnd 1:** Sc 2 in each st around. (12 sts)

**Rnd 2:** *Sc 1, sc 2 in next st; rep from * 5 more times. (18 sts)

**Rnd 3:** *Sc 2, sc 2 in next st; rep from * 5 more times. (24 sts)

**Rnd 4:** *Sc 3, sc 2 in next st; rep from * 5 more times. (30 sts)

**Rnds 5–6:** Sc 30.

**Rnd 7:** *Sc 3, sc2tog; rep from * 5 more times. (24 sts)

**Rnd 8:** *Sc 2, sc2tog; rep from * 5 more times. (18 sts)

**Rnd 9:** *Sc 1, sc2tog; rep from * 5 more times. (12 sts)

Stuff tire.

**Rnd 10:** Sc2tog 6 times. (6 sts)

Fasten off yarn, leaving a long tail for sewing. Close the 6-st hole. Thread the yarn tail back and forth through the center of the tire 3 to 4 times, pulling tightly as you sew to shape the tire.

## HUBCAP (MAKE 2)

Using light gray, make a 6-st adjustable ring.

**Rnd 1:** Sc 2 in each st around. (12 sts)

Cut yarn and fasten off, leaving a long tail for sewing.

Sew the hubcaps to the sides of the tires.

## FENDER (MAKE 2)

Using yellow, make a 6-st adjustable ring.

**Rnd 1:** Sc 2 in each st around. (12 sts)

**Rnds 2–17:** Sc 12.

**Rnd 18:** Sc2tog 6 times. (6 sts)

Fasten off yarn, leaving a long tail for sewing.

Close the 6-st hole.

Wrap the front fenders over the top of the tires and secure to the sides and top of the tire with a few

stitches. Sew tires onto the sides of the cab. Then sew the inside edge of the fender to the side of the cab.

## ROLLER

Using light gray, make a 6-st adjustable ring.

**Rnd 1:** Sc 2 in each st around. (12 sts)

**Rnd 2:** *Sc 1, sc 2 in next st; rep from * 5 more times. (18 sts)

**Rnd 3:** *Sc 2, sc 2 in next st; rep from * 5 more times. (24 sts)

**Rnd 4:** *Sc 3, sc 2 in next st; rep from * 5 more times. (30 sts)

**Rnd 5:** *Sc 4, sc 2 in next st; rep from * 5 more times. (36 sts)

**Rnd 6:** *Sc 5, sc 2 in next st; rep from * 5 more times. (42 sts)

**Rnd 7:** Bpsc 42.

**Rnds 8–27:** Sc 42.

**Rnd 28:** Bpsc 42.

**Rnd 29:** *Sc 5, sc2tog; rep from * 5 more times. (36 sts)

**Rnd 30:** *Sc 4, sc2tog; rep from * 5 more times. (30 sts)

**Rnd 31:** *Sc 3, sc2tog; rep from * 5 more times. (24 sts)

Using foam stabilizer, cut out (1) 12 x 5-inch (31 x 13cm) rectangle. With needle and thread, sew the 5-inch (13cm) edges together to form a tube. Insert foam tube into roller for firmer shaping.

**Rnd 32:** *Sc 2, sc2tog; rep from * 5 more times. (18 sts)

**Rnd 33:** *Sc 1, sc2tog; rep from * 5 more times. (12 sts)

Firmly stuff foam tube inside roller with fiberfill.

**Rnd 34:** Sc2tog 6 times.

Cut yarn, fasten off, and close hole, weaving in end.

## AXLE PIN (MAKE 2)

In dark gray, make a 6-st adjustable ring.

**Rnd 1:** In bl; sc 6. (6 sts)

**Rnd 2:** Sc2tog 3 times. (3 sts)

Fasten off yarn, leaving a long tail.

Cinch hole closed with yarn tail. Thread the yarn tail back and forth through the center of the axle pin 3 to 4 times, pulling tightly as you sew to flatten the axle pin.

## ROLLER BAR

In yellow, loosely ch 61.

**Row 1:** Starting in 2nd ch from hook and working in back ridge loops, sc 60, turn. (60 sts)

**Rows 2–4:** Ch 1, sc 60, turn. (60 sts)

**Row 5:** Ch 1, bl; sc 60, turn. (60 sts)

**Row 6:** Ch 1, fl; sc 60, turn. (60 sts)

**Rows 7–9:** Ch 1, sc 60, turn. (60 sts)

**Row 10:** Ch 1, fl; sc 60. (60 sts)

Cut yarn and fasten off, leaving a long tail for sewing.

Using foam stabilizer, cut out (1) 1 x 18-inch (3 x 46cm) strip. With the surface loops from rows 5, 6, and 10 on the RS, place foam against WS of work. Match up row 1 and row 10 and sew tog with a mattress stitch.

Wrap roller bar around the front and sides of the roller, leaving the ends loose.

Take one axle pin and draw its yarn tail through the side of the roller bar and through the center of one side of the roller. Draw the yarn through the roller to the opposite side and leave loose. Rep on the other side of the roller. Pull gently and secure the yarn tails at the bases of the axle pins.

Sew the ends of the roller bars to the middle of the cab sides below the windows.

Weave in any remaining yarn tails.

# CRANE

**FINISHED SIZE:** 9 x 9 x 16 in. (23 x 23 x 41cm) //// **YARN WEIGHT:**

Picking up building materials with the greatest of ease, Crane is ready to load crates (page **108**) with help from Flatbed Truck (page **16**) to keep the job site neat and tidy. Complete with working crane arm, moving hook, pivoting base, and chunky tracks, this crane is sure to please any heavy machinery enthusiast!

## MATERIALS & TOOLS

- Bulky-weight yarn in black (100 yds/91m), dark gray (150 yds/137m), light gray (300 yds/274m), red (300 yds/274m), and white (300 yds/274m)
- Hook size I (5.5mm)
- Place marker
- Scissors
- Tapestry needle
- Polyester fiberfill
- 1-in. (25mm)-thick cushion foam
- Foam stabilizer
- (1) Black or gray pipe cleaner

## INSTRUCTIONS

### CAB

Starting with red, loosely ch 6.

**Rnd 1:** Starting in 2nd ch and working in back ridge loops, sc 4, sc 4 in next ch. Rotate chain so front side of chain is facing up. Starting in front side of the next ch, sc 3, sc 3 in front side of next ch. (14 sts)

**Rnd 2:** Sc 3 in next st, sc 3, sc 3 in next st, sc 2, sc 3 in next st, sc 3, sc 3 in next st, sc 2. (22 sts)

**Rnd 3:** Sc 1, sc 3 in next st, sc 5, sc 3 in next st, sc 4, sc 3 in next st, sc 5, sc 3 in next st, sc 3. (30 sts)

**Rnd 4:** Sc 2, sc 3 in next st, sc 7, sc 3 in next st, sc 6, sc 3 in next st, sc 7, sc 3 in next st, sc 4. (38 sts)

# CRANE ////

**Rnd 5:** Sc 3, sc 3 in next st, sc 9, sc 3 in next st, sc 8, sc 3 in next st, sc 9, sc 3 in next st, sc 5. (46 sts)

## Cab back wall

To begin: Sl st 5, turn.

**Row 1:** Ch 1, in fl; sc 10. Pm in next st. Turn work. (10 sts)

**Rows 2–8:** Ch 1, sc 10, turn. (10 sts)

Leave yarn tails on front side of work on row 9.

**Row 9:** Ch 1, sc 1, cut red, leaving a 60-inch (1.5m) tail to work with, change to white, sc2tog, sc 4, sc2tog, rejoin red yarn from skein, sc 1, turn. (8 sts)

**Rows 10–14:** Ch 1, sc 1, change to white, sc 6, change to red, sc 1, turn. (8 sts)

Cut white.

**Row 15:** Ch 1, sc2tog, sc 4, sc2tog, turn. (6 sts)

**Row 16:** Ch 1, sc 6, turn. (6 sts)

Cut yarn and fasten off, leaving a long tail for sewing.

## Side wall 1

**Row 1:** Starting with red, (sl st, ch 1, sc 1) in fl of pm stitch to re-attach yarn. Cont working in fl; sc 12. Pm in next st. Turn work. (13 sts)

**Rows 2–3:** Ch 1, sc 13, turn. (13 sts)

Leave yarn tails on back side of work on row 4.

**Row 4:** Ch 1, sc 1, cut red, leaving a 60-inch (1.5m) tail to work with, change to white, sc 11, rejoin red from skein, sc 1, turn. (13 sts)

**Row 5:** Ch 1, sc 1, change to white, sc 11, change to red, sc 1, turn. (13 sts)

**Row 6:** Ch 1, sc 1, change to white, sc2tog, sc 9, change to red, sc 1, turn. (12 sts)

**Rows 7–8:** Ch 1, sc 1, change to white, sc 10, change to red, sc 1, turn. (12 sts)

**Row 9:** Ch 1, sc 1, change to white, sc 8, sc2tog, change to red, sc 1, turn. (11 sts)

**Rows 10–11:** Ch 1, sc 1, change to white, sc 9, change to red, sc 1, turn. (11 sts)

**Row 12:** Ch 1, sc 1, change to white, sc2tog, sc 7, change to red, sc 1, turn. (10 sts)

**Rows 13–14:** Ch 1, sc 1, change to white, sc 8, change to red, sc 1, turn. (10 sts)

Cut white.

**Row 15:** Ch 1, sc 8, sc2tog, turn. (9 sts)

**Row 16:** Ch 1, sc 9, turn. (9 sts)

Cut yarn and fasten off, leaving a long tail for sewing.

## Cab front wall

**Row 1:** Starting with red, (sl st, ch 1, sc 1) in fl of pm stitch to re-attach yarn. Cont working in fl; sc 9, pm in next st. Turn work. (10 sts)

**Rows 2–3:** Ch 1, sc 10, turn. (10 sts)

Leave yarn tails on back side of work on row 4.

**Row 4:** Ch 1, sc 1, cut red, leaving a 60-inch (1.5m) tail to work with, change to white, sc 8, rejoin red from skein, sc 1, turn. (10 sts)

**Rows 5–8:** Ch 1, sc 1, change to white, sc 8, change to red, sc 1, turn. (10 sts)

**Row 9:** Ch 1, sc 1, change to white, sc2tog, sc 4, sc2tog, change to red, sc 1, turn. (8 sts)

Cont with cab back wall starting at row 10.

## Side wall 2

**Row 1:** Starting with red, (sl st, ch 1, sc 1) in fl of pm stitch to re-attach yarn. Cont working in fl; sc 12. Turn work. (13 sts)

**Rows 2–3:** Ch 1, sc 13, turn. (13 sts)

Leave yarn tails on back side of work on row 4.

**Row 4:** Ch 1, sc 1, cut red, leaving a 72-inch (1.8m) tail to work with, change to white, sc 11, rejoin red from skein, sc 1, turn. (13 sts)

**Row 5:** Ch 1, sc 1, change to white, sc 11, change to red, sc 1, turn. (13 sts)

**Row 6:** Ch 1, sc 1, change to white, sc 9, sc2tog, change to red, sc 1, turn. (12 sts)

**Rows 7–8:** Ch 1, sc 1, change to white, sc 10, change to red, sc 1, turn. (12 sts)

**Row 9:** Ch 1, sc 1, change to white, sc2tog, sc 8, change to red, sc 1, turn. (11 sts)

**Rows 10–11:** Ch 1, sc 1, change to white, sc 9, change to red, sc 1, turn. (11 sts)

**Row 12:** Ch 1, sc 1, change to white, sc 7, sc2tog, change to red, sc 1, turn. (10 sts)

**Rows 13–14:** Ch 1, sc 1, change to white, sc 8, change to red, sc 1, turn. (10 sts)

Cut white.

**Row 15:** Ch 1, sc2tog, sc 8, turn. (9 sts)

**Row 16:** Ch 1, sc 9, turn. (9 sts)

Cut yarn and fasten off, leaving a long tail for sewing.

Sew up side edges. Using 1-inch (25mm)-thick cushion foam, cut out (1) 4½ x 3-inch (10 x 8cm) rectangle and place at bottom of cab. Stuff the rest of the cab with fiberfill.

## CAB ROOF

In red, loosely ch 6.

**Rnd 1:** Starting in 2nd ch and working in back ridge loops, sc 4, sc 4 in next ch. Rotate chain so front side of chain is facing up. Starting in front side of the next ch, sc 3, sc 3 in front side of next ch. (14 sts)

**Rnd 2:** Sc 3 in next st, sc 3, sc 3 in next st, sc 2, sc 3 in next st, sc 3, sc 3 in next st, sc 2. (22 sts)

**Rnd 3:** Sc 1, sc 3 in next st, sc 5, sc 3 in next st, sc 4, sc 3 in next st, sc 5, sc 3 in next st, sc 3. (30 sts)

**Rnd 4:** Sc 2, sc 3 in next st, sc 7 sc 3 in next st, sc 6, sc 3 in next st, sc 7, sc 3 in next st, sc 4. (38 sts)

**Rnd 5:** Sc 3, sc 3 in next st, sc 9, sc 3 in next st, sc 8, sc 3 in next st, sc 9, sc 3 in next st, sc 5. (46 sts)

**Rnd 6:** In bl; sc 46. (46 sts)

**Rnd 7:** In bl; sc 3, sc3tog, sc 9, sc3tog, sc 8, sc3tog, sc 9, sc3tog, sc 5. (38 sts)

**Rnd 8:** Sc 2, sc3tog, sc 7, sc3tog, sc 6, sc3tog, sc 7, sc3tog, sc 4. (30 sts)

**Rnd 9:** Sc 1, sc3tog, sc 5, sc3tog, sc 4, sc3tog, sc 5, sc3tog, sc 3. (22 sts)

Using foam stabilizer, cut out (1) 3¼ x 3-inch (8 x 8cm) rectangle. Insert foam into roof.

# CRANE ////

**Rnd 10:** Sc3tog, sc 3, sc3tog, sc 2, sc3tog, sc 3, sc3tog, sc 2. (14 sts)

**Rnd 11:** Sc 14. (14 sts)

Cut yarn and fasten off, leaving a long tail for sewing.

Sew the roof seam closed. With roof seam side down, sew bottom edge of roof to the open edge of the cab. Add more stuffing if needed before closing seam.

## REAR ENGINE

With red, loosely ch 10.

**Rnd 1:** Starting in 2nd ch and working in back ridge loops, sc 8, sc 4 in next ch. Rotate chain so front side of chain is facing up. Starting in front side of the next ch, sc 7, sc 3 in front side of next ch. (22 sts)

**Rnd 2:** Sc 3 in next st, sc 7, sc 3 in next st, sc 2, sc 3 in next st, sc 7, sc 3 in next st, sc 2. (30 sts)

**Rnd 3:** Sc 1, sc 3 in next st, sc 9, sc 3 in next st, sc 4, sc 3 in next st, sc 9, sc 3 in next st, sc 3. (38 sts)

**Rnd 4:** Sc 2, sc 3 in next st, sc 11, sc 3 in next st, sc 6, sc 3 in next st, sc 11, sc 3 in next st, sc 4. (46 sts)

**Rnd 5:** Sc 3, sc 3 in next st, sc 13, sc 3 in next st, sc 8, sc 3 in next st, sc 13, sc 3 in next st, sc 5. (54 sts)

### Rear engine back wall

To begin: Sl st 5, turn.

**Row 1:** Ch 1, in fl; sc 10. Pm in next st. Turn work. (10 sts)

**Rows 2–8:** Ch 1, sc 10, turn. (10 sts)

Cut yarn and fasten off, leaving a long tail for sewing.

### Side wall 1

**Row 1:** With red, (sl st, ch 1, sc 1) in fl of pm stitch to re-attach yarn. Cont working in fl; sc 16. Pm in next st. Turn work. (17 sts)

**Rows 2–8:** Ch 1, sc 17, turn. (17 sts)

Cut yarn and fasten off, leaving a long tail for sewing.

### Front wall and roof

**Row 1:** With red, (sl st, ch 1, sc 1) in fl of pm stitch to re-attach yarn. Cont working in fl; sc 9, pm in next st. Turn work. (10 sts)

**Rows 2–8:** Ch 1, sc 10, turn. (10 sts)

**Row 9:** In fl; sc 10, turn.

**Rows 10–26:** Ch 1, sc 10, turn. (10 sts)

### Side wall 2

**Row 1:** With red, (sl st, ch 1, sc 1) in fl of pm stitch to re-attach yarn. Cont working in fl; sc 16. Pm in next st. Turn work. (17 sts)

**Rows 2–8:** Ch 1, sc 17, turn. (17 sts)

Cut yarn and fasten off, leaving a long tail for sewing.

Sew the short edges of the rear engine together. Leave the roof flap open. Using 1-inch (25mm)-thick cushion foam, cut out (3) 3 x 4-inch (8 x 10cm) rectangles. Stack the foam into a block shape. Place foam block inside rear engine. Sew the seam closed around the roof edge of the rear engine.

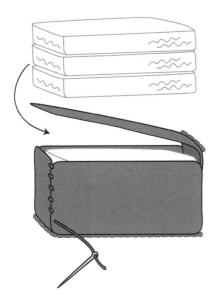

## PLATFORM

With red, loosely ch 73.

**Row 1:** Starting in 2nd ch from hook, sc 72, turn. (72 sts)

**Rows 2–3:** Ch 1, sc 72, turn. (72 sts)

Cut yarn and fasten off, leaving a long tail for sewing. Turn work.

**Row 4:** Count 28 sts in from end. Working in fl of 28 st (sl st 1, ch 1, sc 1). Cont to work down the row in fl; sc 17 and leave remaining sts unworked. Turn. (18 sts)

**Rows 5–36:** Ch 1, sc 18, turn. (18 sts)

**Row 37:** Ch 1, in bl; sc 18, turn. (18 sts)

**Rows 38–39:** Ch 1, sc 18, turn. (18 sts)

**Row 40:** Ch 1, in fl; sc 18, turn. (18 sts)

**Rows 41–72:** Ch 1, sc 18, turn. (18 sts)

Cut yarn and fasten off, leaving a long tail for sewing.

With the surface loops of the platform facing out, sew row 72 to the middle of row 1.

Using 1-inch (25mm)-thick cushion foam, cut out (1) 5 x 8 ¾-inch (13 x 22cm) rectangle. Insert foam between the top and bottom layers of the platform. Pin side edges in place and sew edges together with a whip stitch.

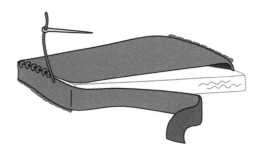

Sew cab and rear engine to platform with drive side of cab lined up with edge of platform.

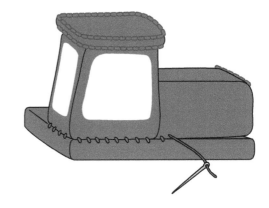

Double up dark gray yarn on tapestry needle and embroider a chain stitch around the edges of the cab windows. On side of rear engine, embroider 2 chain stitch squares (refer to photo on page 62 for reference).

## ROLLER BASE (MAKE 2)

With dark gray, loosely ch 20.

**Rnd 1:** Starting in 2nd ch and working in back ridge loops, sc 18, sc 4 in next ch. Rotate chain so front side of chain is facing up. Starting in front side of the next ch, sc 17, sc 3 in front side of next ch. (42 sts)

**Rnd 2:** Sc 2 in next st, sc 17, sc 2 in next 4 sts, sc 17, sc 2 in next 3 sts. (50 sts)

**Rnd 3:** Sc 2 in next st, sc 21, sc 2 in next 4 sts, sc 21, sc 2 in next 3 sts. (58 sts)

**Rnd 4:** In bl; sc 58. (58 sts)

**Rnds 5–6:** Sc 58. (58 sts)

**Rnd 7:** In bl; sc2tog, sc 21, sc2tog 4 times, sc 21, sc2tog 3 times. (50 sts)

# CRANE ////

**Rnd 8:** Sc2tog, sc 17, sc2tog 4 times, sc 17, sc2tog 3 times. (42 sts)

**Rnd 9:** Sc 42. (42 sts)

Cut yarn and fasten off, leaving a long tail. Stuff and close seam.

## ROLLER (MAKE 10)

With light gray, make a 4-st adjustable ring.

**Rnd 1:** Sc 2 in each st around. (8 sts)

Cut yarn and fasten off, leaving a long tail for sewing.

Starting with the center roller, sew 5 rollers to the front of the roller base along the bottom edge. Rep on other base (refer to photos for reference).

## TRACK (MAKE 2)

In black, loosely ch 7, turn.

**Row 1:** Starting in 2nd ch from hook, sc 6, turn. (6 sts)

**Row 2:** Ch 1, sc 6, turn. (6 sts)

**Row 3:** Ch 1, sk 1, FPsc around the 5 stitch posts, turn.

**Row 4:** Working in the tops of the 6 sts of row 3 (directly in front of the FPsc sts), ch 1, sc 6, turn. (6 sts)

**Row 5:** Ch 1, sc 6, turn. (6 sts)

**Row 6:** Ch 1, sk 1, BPsc around the next 5 stitch posts, turn.

**Row 7:** Working in the tops of the 6 exposed sts of row 6 (directly in back of the BPsc sts), ch 1, sc 6, turn. (6 sts)

Rep rows 2–7 11 more times until you have 24 ridges.

Sc along 1 long edge (this will become the outside edge of the track). Sl st along short edge and then along remaining long edge (this will become the inside edge of the track). Cut yarn and fasten off, leaving a long tail for sewing.

To complete the track and roller unit, sew the short edges of the track together to create a loop. With the

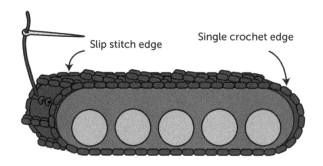

Slip stitch edge

Single crochet edge

sc edge facing out, slip the loop over the roller base. With the roller detail facing out, sew the sl st edge to the back edge of the roller base.

## BASE PIVOT

Using dark gray, make a 6-st adjustable ring.

**Rnd 1:** Sc 2 in each st around. (12 sts)

**Rnd 2:** *Sc 1, sc 2 in next st; rep from * 5 more times. (18 sts)

**Rnd 3:** *Sc 2, sc 2 in next st; rep from * 5 more times. (24 sts)

**Rnd 4:** *Sc 3, sc 2 in next st; rep from * 5 more times. (30 sts)

**Rnds 5–6:** Sc 30.

**Rnd 7:** *Sc 3, sc2tog; rep from * 5 more times. (24 sts)

**Rnd 8:** *Sc 2, sc2tog; rep from * 5 more times. (18 sts)

**Rnd 9:** *Sc 1, sc2tog; rep from * 5 more times. (12 sts)

Stuff base pivot.

**Rnd 10:** Sc2tog 6 times. (6 sts)

Fasten off yarn, leaving a long tail for sewing. Close the 6-st hole.

## BASE

Using dark gray, loosely ch 53.

**Row 1:** Starting in 2nd ch from hook, sc 52, turn. (52 sts)

**Rows 2–3:** Ch 1, sc 52, turn. (52 sts)

Cut yarn and fasten off, leaving a long tail for sewing. Turn work.

**Row 4:** Count 22 sts in from end. Working in fl of 22nd st (sl st 1, ch 1, sc 1). Cont to work down the row in fl; sc 9 and leave remaining sts unworked. Turn. (10 sts)

**Rows 5–27:** Ch 1, sc 10, turn. (10 sts)

**Row 28:** Ch 1, in fl; sc 10, turn. (10 sts)

**Rows 29–30:** Ch 1, sc 10, turn. (10 sts)

**Row 31:** Ch 1, in bl; sc 10, turn. (10 sts)

**Rows 32–53:** Ch 1, sc 10, turn. (10 sts)

Cut yarn and fasten off, leaving a long tail for sewing.

With the surface loops of the base facing out, sew row 53 to the middle of row 1.

Using 1-inch (25mm)-thick cushion foam, cut out (1) 3 x 6-inch (8 x 15cm) rectangle. Insert foam pieces between the top and bottom layers of the base. Pin side edges in place and sew edges together with a whip stitch.

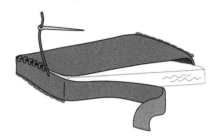

With dark gray, attach yarn to the middle of one side of the base. Draw yarn through the base and then through the base pivot. Finally, draw the yarn up through the middle of the platform. Re-insert the needle into the platform, following the path of the yarn down to the attachment point. Pull tightly to bring the three pieces close together and secure yarn to the bottom of the roller base.

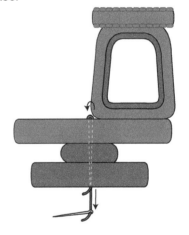

Sew the side edge of the base to the back sides of the roller bases.

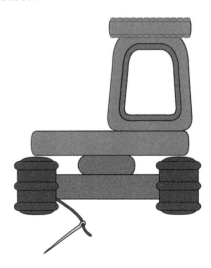

# CRANE ////

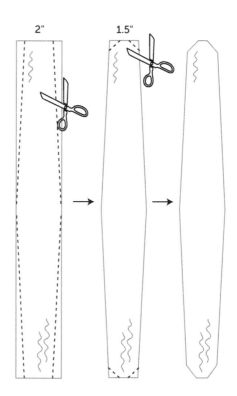

## CRANE ARM

Starting with white, loosely ch 46.

**Rnd 1:** Starting in 2nd ch and working in back ridge loops, sc 44, sc 4 in next ch. Rotate chain so front side of chain is facing up. Starting in front side of the next ch, sc 43, sc 3 in front side of next ch. (94 sts)

**Rnd 2:** Sc 2 in next st, sc 10, hdc 9, dc 5, hdc 9, sc 10, sc 2 in next 4 sts, sc 10, hdc 9, dc 5, hdc 9, sc 10, sc 2 in next 3 sts. (102 sts)

Change to red.

**Rnd 3:** Sc 2 in next st, sc 47, sc 2 in next 4 sts, sc 47, sc 2 in next 3 sts. (110 sts)

**Rnd 4:** In bl; sc 110. (110 sts)

**Rnd 5:** Sc 110. (110 sts)

**Rnd 6:** In bl; sc2tog, sc 47, sc2tog 4 times, sc 47, sc2tog 3 times. (102 sts)

Change to white.

**Rnd 7:** Sc2tog, sc 10, hdc 9, dc 5, hdc 9, sc 10, sc2tog 4 times, sc 10, hdc 9, dc 5, hdc 9, sc 10, sc2tog 3 times. (94 sts)

**Rnd 8:** Sc 94. (94 sts)

Cut yarn and fasten off, leaving a long tail. Stuff and close seam.

Using 1-inch (25mm)-thick cushion foam, cut out (1) 14½ x 2-inch (37 x 5cm) rectangle. From the center, taper

the ends of the rectangle down to 1½ inches (4cm) to make a long diamond-like shape. Clip the 4 corners to round the edges. Insert foam into crane arm and close seam.

Double up red yarn on a tapestry needle and embroider a zigzag design on each side of the crane arm (refer to photos for reference).

> **TIP:** Use marking pins or slip rings to lay out the corners of the zigzag design before you begin to keep everything even.

## CRANE ARM BASE

With red, make an 8-st adjustable ring.

**Rnd 1:** Sc 2 in each st around. (16 sts)

**Rnd 2:** *Sc 1, sc 2 in next st; rep from * around. (24 sts)

**Rnd 3:** *Sc 2, sc 2 in next st; rep from * around. (32 sts)

**Rnd 4:** *Sc 3, sc 2 in next st; rep from * around. (40 sts)

**Rnd 5:** In bl; sc 20 (leave remaining 20 sts unworked). Cut yarn and fasten off, leaving a long tail for sewing.

Using foam stabilizer, cut out (1) 3-inch (8cm) circle. Cut circle in half and place halves together. Fold crane arm base in half so the sc 20 from rnd 5

is on one half. Insert the doubled-up foam semi-circle and sew seams shut.

Sew the flat edge of the semi-circle crane arm base to the back side edge of the platform.

## AXLE PIN (MAKE 1 IN LIGHT GRAY AND 1 IN RED)

In light gray or red, make a 6-st adjustable ring.

**Rnd 1:** In bl; sc 6. (6 sts)

**Rnd 2:** Sc2tog 3 times. (3 sts)

Cut yarn and fasten off, leaving a long tail for sewing.

Cinch hole closed with yarn tail. Thread the yarn tail back and forth through the center of the axle pin 3 to 4 times, pulling tightly as you sew to flatten the axle pin.

Place one end of crane arm in between crane arm base and rear engine. Draw the light gray axle pin yarn tail through the crane arm base, crane arm and catching the side of the rear engine. Draw yarn back out, following the original path of the yarn through the crane arm and crane arm base. Bring yarn out through front of axle pin and pull very tightly to sandwich the crane arm between the crane arm base and rear engine. Secure yarn and sew in yarn tails.

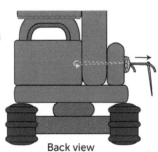

Back view

## HOOK

Starting with light gray, make a 3-st adjustable ring.

**Rnds 1–7:** Sc 3. (3 sts)

Change to red.

**Rnd 8:** Sc 3 in each st around. (9 sts)

**Rnd 9:** *Sc 2, sc 1 in next st; rep from * 2 more times. (12 sts)

**Rnd 10:** Sc 12. (12 sts)

**Rnd 11:** Sc2tog 6 times. (6 sts)

Cut yarn and fasten off, leaving a long tail for sewing.

Fold over a 5 to 6-inch (13 to 15cm) piece of pipe cleaner and twist the ends together to make a flattened loop. Thread yarn through the pipe cleaner loop and onto a tapestry needle. Working from the rnd 11 opening, insert the needle down through the hook and out at rnd 1. Draw the pipe cleaner down through the hook and remove the yarn once it is in position. Curve the hook.

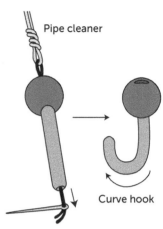

Pipe cleaner

Curve hook

Stuff red part of hook with stuffing and close opening. In light gray, sl st into the top of the hook, then cont to ch until your chain is 9 inches (23cm) long and fasten off. Sew the red axle pin to the end of the chain and weave in loose ends.

## CRANE HOOK STRAP (MAKE 2)

In red, loosely ch 6.

**Row 1:** Starting in 2nd ch from hook, sl st 5, cut yarn, and fasten off, leaving a long tail for sewing.

Sew one strap to the front of the crane arm, then sew the second strap 2 inches (5cm) behind it on the top edge of the crane arm. Slide the red axle pin and light gray chain under the two straps to allow the hook to slide up and down.

Weave in any remaining yarn tails.

> **TIP:** Feel free to sew the crane to the side of the cab in an upright position if you prefer. The arm is rather heavy and even when the pivot point at the base is secure and snug, the arm still tends to droop.

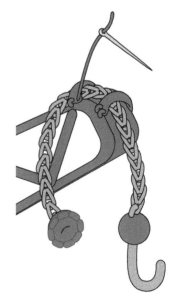

# EXCAVATOR

**FINISHED SIZE:** 12 x 7 x 9 in. (30 x 18 x 23cm) /// **YARN WEIGHT:**

A favorite on the job site, Excavator is ready to get the job done with its oversized working bucket arm, pivoting base, and chunky tracks. This pattern even includes an optional auger attachment to help drill those deep holes needed for putting up extra-tall skyscrapers!

## MATERIALS & TOOLS

- Bulky-weight yarn in black (100 yds/91m), dark gray (150 yds/137m), light gray (300 yds/274m), white (150 yds/137m), and yellow (300 yds/274m)
- Hook size I (5.5mm)
- Place marker
- Scissors
- Tapestry needle
- Polyester fiberfill
- 1-in. (25mm)-thick cushion foam
- Foam stabilizer

## INSTRUCTIONS

### CAB

Starting with yellow, loosely ch 6.

**Rnd 1:** Starting in 2nd ch and working in back ridge loops, sc 4, sc 4 in next ch. Rotate chain so front side of chain is facing up. Starting in front side of the next ch, sc 3, sc 3 in front side of next ch. (14 sts)

**Rnd 2:** Sc 3 in next st, sc 3, sc 3 in next st, sc 2, sc 3 in next st, sc 3, sc 3 in next st, sc 2. (22 sts)

**Rnd 3:** Sc 1, sc 3 in next st, sc 5, sc 3 in next st, sc 4, sc 3 in next st, sc 5, sc 3 in next st, sc 3. (30 sts)

**Rnd 4:** Sc 2, sc 3 in next st, sc 7, sc 3 in next st, sc 6, sc 3 in next st, sc 7, sc 3 in next st, sc 4. (38 sts)

**Rnd 5:** Sc 3, sc 3 in next st, sc 9, sc 3 in next st, sc 8, sc 3 in next st, sc 9, sc 3 in next st, sc 5. (46 sts)

## Cab back wall

To begin: Sl st 5, turn.

**Row 1:** Ch 1, in fl; sc 10. Pm in next st. Turn work. (10 sts)

**Rows 2–8:** Ch 1, sc 10, turn. (10 sts)

Cut yellow, change to black. Leave yarn tails in front of work on row 9.

**Row 9:** Ch 1, sc 1, cut black, leaving a 60-inch (1.5m) tail to work with, change to white, sc2tog, sc 4, sc2tog, rejoin black yarn from skein, sc 1, turn. (8 sts)

**Rows 10–14:** Ch 1, sc 1, change to white, sc 6, change to black, sc 1, turn. (8 sts)

Cut white.

**Row 15:** Ch 1, sc2tog, sc 4, sc2tog, turn. (6 sts)

**Row 16:** Ch 1, sc 6, turn. (6 sts)

Cut yarn and fasten off, leaving a long tail for sewing.

## Side wall 1

**Row 1:** Starting with yellow, (sl st, ch 1, sc 1) in fl of pm stitch to re-attach yarn. Cont working in fl; sc 12. Pm in next st. Turn work. (13 sts)

**Rows 2–3:** Ch 1, sc 13, turn. (13 sts)

Cut yellow, change to black. Leave yarn tails in backside of work on row 4.

**Row 4:** Ch 1, sc 1, cut black, leaving a 60-inch (1.5m) tail to work with, change to white, sc 11, rejoin black from skein, sc 1, turn. (13 sts)

**Row 5:** Ch 1, sc 1, change to white, sc 11, change to black, sc 1, turn. (13 sts)

**Row 6:** Ch 1, sc 1, change to white, sc2tog, sc 9, change to black, sc 1, turn. (12 sts)

**Rows 7–8:** Ch 1, sc 1, change to white, sc 10, change to black, sc 1, turn. (12 sts)

**Row 9:** Ch 1, sc 1, change to white, sc 8, sc2tog, change to black, sc 1, turn. (11 sts)

**Rows 10–11:** Ch 1, sc 1, change to white, sc 9, change to black, sc 1, turn. (11 sts)

**Row 12:** Ch 1, sc 1, change to white, sc2tog, sc 7, change to black, sc 1, turn. (10 sts)

**Rows 13–14:** Ch 1, sc 1, change to white, sc 8, change to black, sc 1, turn. (10 sts)

Cut white.

**Row 15:** Ch 1, sc 8, sc2tog, turn. (9 sts)

**Row 16:** Ch 1, sc 9, turn. (9 sts)

Cut yarn and fasten off, leaving a long tail for sewing.

### Front cab wall

**Row 1:** Starting with yellow, (sl st, ch 1, sc 1) in fl of pm stitch to re-attach yarn. Cont working in fl; sc 9, pm in next st. Turn work. (10 sts)

**Rows 2–3:** Ch 1, sc 10, turn. (10 sts)

Cut yellow, change to black. Leave yarn tails on backside of work on row 4.

**Row 4:** Ch 1, sc 1, cut black, leaving a 60-inch (1.5m) tail to work with, change to white, sc 8, rejoin black from skein, sc 1, turn. (10 sts)

**Rows 5–8:** Ch 1, sc 1, change to white, sc 8, change to black, sc 1, turn. (10 sts)

**Row 9:** Ch 1, sc 1, change to white, sc2tog, sc 4, sc2tog, change to black, sc 1, turn. (8 sts)

Starting at row 10, repeat cab back wall.

### Side wall 2

**Row 1:** Starting with yellow, (sl st, ch 1, sc 1) in fl of pm stitch to re-attach yarn. Cont working in fl; sc 12. Turn work. (13 sts)

**Rows 2–3:** Ch 1, sc 13, turn. (13 sts)

Cut yellow, change to black. Leave yarn tails in backside of work on row 4.

**Row 4:** Ch 1, sc 1, cut black, leaving a 60-inch (1.5m) tail to work with, change to white, sc 11, rejoin black from skein, sc 1, turn. (13 sts)

**Row 5:** Ch 1, sc 1, change to white, sc 11, change to black, sc 1, turn. (13 sts)

**Row 6:** Ch 1, sc 1, change to white, sc 9, sc2tog, change to black, sc 1, turn. (12 sts)

**Rows 7–8:** Ch 1, sc 1, change to white, sc 10, change to black, sc 1, turn. (12 sts)

**Row 9:** Ch 1, sc 1, change to white, sc2tog, sc 8, change to black, sc 1, turn. (11 sts)

**Rows 10–11:** Ch 1, sc 1, change to white, sc 9, change to black, sc 1, turn. (11 sts)

**Row 12:** Ch 1, sc 1, change to white, sc 7, sc2tog, change to black, sc 1, turn. (10 sts)

**Rows 13–14:** Ch 1, sc 1, change to white, sc 8, change to black, sc 1, turn. (10 sts)

**Cut white.**

**Row 15:** Ch 1, sc2tog, sc 8, turn. (9 sts)

**Row 16:** Ch 1, sc 9, turn. (9 sts)

Cut yarn and fasten off, leaving a long tail for sewing.

Sew up side edges.

Using 1-inch (25mm)-thick cushion foam, cut out (1) 4 ½ x 3-inch (11 x 8cm) rectangle and place at bottom of cab. Stuff the rest of the cab with fiberfill.

## CAB ROOF

In yellow, loosely ch 6.

**Rnd 1:** Starting in 2nd ch and working in back ridge loops, sc 4, sc 4 in next ch. Rotate chain so front side of chain is facing up. Starting in front side of the next ch, sc 3, sc 3 in front side of next ch. (14 sts)

**Rnd 2:** Sc 3 in next st, sc 3, sc 3 in next st, sc 2, sc 3 in next st, sc 3, sc 3 in next st, sc 2. (22 sts)

# EXCAVATOR ////

**Rnd 3:** Sc 1, sc 3 in next st, sc 5, sc 3 in next st, sc 4, sc 3 in next st, sc 5, sc 3 in next st, sc 3. (30 sts)

**Rnd 4:** Sc 2, sc 3 in next st, sc 7, sc 3 in next st, sc 6, sc 3 in next st, sc 7, sc 3 in next st, sc 4. (38 sts)

**Rnd 5:** Sc 3, sc 3 in next st, sc 9, sc 3 in next st, sc 8, sc 3 in next st, sc 9, sc 3 in next st, sc 5. (46 sts)

**Rnd 6:** In bl; sc 46. (46 sts)

**Rnd 7:** In bl; sc 3, sc3tog, sc 9, sc3tog, sc 8, sc3tog, sc 9, sc3tog, sc 5. (38 sts)

**Rnd 8:** Sc 2, sc3tog, sc 7, sc3tog, sc 6, sc3tog, sc 7, sc3tog, sc 4. (30 sts)

**Rnd 9:** Sc 1, sc3tog, sc 5, sc3tog, sc 4, sc3tog, sc 5, sc3tog, sc 3. (22 sts)

Using foam stabilizer, cut out (1) 3¼ x 3-inch (8 x 8cm) rectangle. Insert foam into roof.

**Rnd 10:** Sc3tog, sc 3, sc3tog, sc 2, sc3tog, sc 3, sc3tog, sc 2. (14 sts)

**Rnd 11:** Sc 14. (14 sts)

Cut yarn and fasten off, leaving a long tail for sewing.

Sew the roof seam closed. With roof seam side down, sew bottom edge of roof to the open edge of the cab. Add more stuffing if needed before closing seam.

## REAR ENGINE

In yellow, loosely ch 6.

**Rnd 1:** Starting in 2nd ch and working in back ridge loops, sc 4, sc 4 in next ch. Rotate chain so front side of chain is facing up. Starting in front side of the next ch, sc 3, sc 3 in front side of next ch. (14 sts)

**Rnd 2:** Sc 3 in next st, sc 3, sc 3 in next st, sc 2, sc 3 in next st, sc 3, sc 3 in next st, sc 2. (22 sts)

**Rnd 3:** Sc 1, sc 3 in next st, sc 5, sc 3 in next st, sc 4, sc 3 in next st, sc 5, sc 3 in next st, sc 3. (30 sts)

**Rnd 4:** Sc 2, sc 3 in next st, sc 7, sc 3 in next st, sc 6, sc 3 in next st, sc 7, sc 3 in next st, sc 4. (38 sts)

**Rnd 5:** Sc 3, sc 3 in next st, sc 9, sc 3 in next st, sc 8, sc 3 in next st, sc 9, sc 3 in next st, sc 5. (46 sts)

### Rear engine back wall

To begin: Sl st 5, turn.

**Row 1:** Ch 1, in fl; sc 10. Pm in next st. Turn work. (10 sts)

**Rows 2–8:** Ch 1, sc 10, turn. (10 sts)

Cut yarn and fasten off, leaving a long tail for sewing.

### Side wall 1

**Row 1:** With yellow, (sl st, ch 1, sc 1) in fl of pm stitch to re-attach yarn. Cont working in fl; sc 12. Pm in next st. Turn work. (13 sts)

**Rows 2–8:** Ch 1, sc 13, turn. (13 sts)

Cut yarn and fasten off, leaving a long tail for sewing.

### Front wall and roof

**Row 1:** With yellow, (sl st, ch 1, sc 1) in fl of pm stitch to re-attach yarn. Cont working in fl; sc 9. Pm in next st. Turn work. (10 sts)

**Rows 2–8:** Ch 1, sc 10, turn. (10 sts)

**Row 9:** In fl; sc 10, turn. (10 sts)

**Rows 10–21:** Ch 1, sc 10, turn. (10 sts)

Cut yarn and fasten off, leaving a long tail for sewing.

### Side wall 2

**Row 1:** With yellow, (sl st, ch 1, sc 1) in fl of pm stitch to re-attach yarn. Cont working in fl; sc 12. Pm in next st. Turn work. (13 sts)

**Rows 2–8:** Ch 1, sc 13, turn. (13 sts)

Cut yarn and fasten off, leaving a long tail for sewing.

Sew the short edges of the rear engine together. Leave the roof flap open. Using 1-inch (25mm)-thick cushion foam, cut out (3) 3 x 4-inch (8 x 10cm) rectangles. Stack foam to make block. Place inside rear engine. Sew seam closed around roof edge of rear engine.

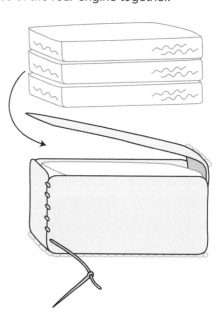

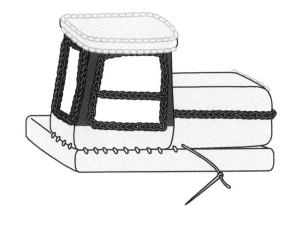

## PLATFORM

With yellow, loosely ch 63.

**Row 1:** Starting in 2nd ch from hook, sc 62, turn. (62 sts)

**Rows 2–3:** Ch 1, sc 62, turn. (62 sts)

Cut yarn and fasten off, leaving a long tail for sewing. Turn work.

**Row 4:** Count 23 sts in from end. Working in fl of 23rd (sl st 1, ch 1, sc 1). Cont to work down the row in fl; sc 17 and leave remaining sts unworked. Turn. (18 sts)

**Rows 5–30:** Ch 1, sc 18, turn. (18 sts)

**Row 31:** Ch 1, in bl; sc 18, turn. (18 sts)

**Rows 32–33:** Ch 1, sc 18, turn. (18 sts)

**Row 34:** Ch 1, in fl; sc 18, turn. (18 sts)

**Rows 35–60:** Ch 1, sc 18, turn. (18 sts)

Cut yarn and fasten off, leaving a long tail for sewing.

With the surface loops of the platform facing out, sew row 60 to the middle of row 1.

Using 1-inch (25mm)-thick cushion foam, cut out (1) 5 x 7 ½-inch (13 x 19cm) rectangle. Insert foam between the top and bottom layers of the platform. Pin side edges in place and sew edges together with a whip stitch.

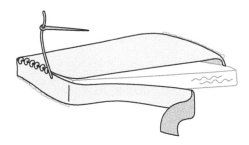

Sew cab and rear engine to platform with driver's side of cab lined up with edge of platform. Double up black yarn on tapestry needle and embroider a chain stitch around the edges of the cab windows, adding a window detail to side windows and a line of stitches around the center of the rear engine (refer to photos for reference).

## BASE PIVOT

Using dark gray, make a 6-st adjustable ring.

**Rnd 1:** Sc 2 in each st around. (12 sts)

**Rnd 2:** *Sc 1, sc 2 in next st; rep from * 5 more times. (18 sts)

**Rnd 3:** *Sc 2, sc 2 in next st; rep from * 5 more times. (24 sts)

**Rnd 4:** *Sc 3, sc 2 in next st; rep from * 5 more times. (30 sts)

**Rnds 5–6:** Sc 30.

**Rnd 7:** *Sc 3, sc2tog; rep from * 5 more times. (24 sts)

**Rnd 8:** *Sc 2, sc2tog; rep from * 5 more times. (18 sts)

**Rnd 9:** *Sc 1, sc2tog; rep from * 5 more times. (12 sts)

Stuff base pivot.

**Rnd 10:** Sc2tog 6 times. (6 sts)

Cut yarn and fasten off, leaving a long tail for sewing. Close the 6-st hole.

## BASE

Using dark gray, loosely ch 43.

**Row 1:** Starting in 2nd ch from hook, sc 42, turn. (42 sts)

**Rows 2–3:** Ch 1, sc 42, turn. (42 sts)

Cut yarn and fasten off, leaving a long tail for sewing. Turn work.

# EXCAVATOR ////

**Row 4:** Count 17 sts in from end. Working in fl of 17th st (sl st 1, ch 1, sc 1). Cont to work down the row in fl; sc 9 and leave remaining sts unworked. Turn. (10 sts)

**Rows 5–19:** Ch 1, sc 10, turn. (10 sts)

**Row 20:** Ch 1, in fl; sc 10, turn. (10 sts)

**Rows 21–22:** Ch 1, sc 10, turn. (10 sts)

**Row 23:** Ch 1, in bl; sc 10, turn. (10 sts)

**Rows 24–37:** Ch 1, sc 10, turn. (10 sts)

Cut yarn and fasten off, leaving a long tail for sewing.

With the surface loops of the excavator base facing out, sew row 37 to the middle of row 1.

Using 1-inch (25mm)-thick cushion foam, cut out (1) 3 x 4-inch (8 x 10cm) rectangle. Insert foam pieces between the top and bottom layers of the base. Pin side edges in place and sew edges together with a whip stitch.

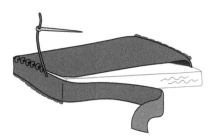

With dark gray, attach yarn to the middle of one side of the base. Draw yarn through the base and then through the base pivot. Finally, draw the yarn up through the middle of the platform. Re-insert the needle into the platform, following the path of the yarn down to the attachment point. Pull tightly to bring the three pieces close together and secure yarn to the bottom of the roller base.

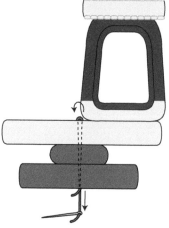

## ROLLER BASE (MAKE 2)

With dark gray, loosely ch 16.

**Rnd 1:** Starting in 2nd ch and working in back ridge loops, sc 14, sc 4 in next ch. Rotate chain so front side of chain is facing up. Starting in front side of the next ch, sc 13, sc 3 in front side of next ch. (34 sts)

**Rnd 2:** Sc 2 in next st, sc 13, sc 2 in next 4 sts, sc 13, sc 2 in next 3 sts. (42 sts)

**Rnd 3:** Sc 2 in next st, sc 17, sc 2 in next 4 sts, sc 17, sc 2 in next 3 sts. (50 sts)

**Rnd 4:** In bl; sc 50. (50 sts)

**Rnds 5–6:** Sc 50. (50 sts)

**Rnd 7:** In bl; sc2tog, sc 17, sc2tog 4 times, sc 17, sc2tog 3 times. (42 sts)

**Rnd 8:** Sc2tog, sc 13, sc2tog 4 times, sc 13, sc2tog 3 times. (34 sts)

**Rnd 9:** Sc 34.

Cut yarn and fasten off, leaving a long tail. Stuff and close seam.

## ROLLER (MAKE 8)

With light gray, make a 4-st adjustable ring.

**Rnd 1:** Sc 2 in each st around. (8 sts)

Cut yarn and fasten off, leaving a long tail for sewing.

Sew 4 rollers to the front of the roller base along the

bottom edge. Rep on other base.

## TRACK (MAKE 2)

In black, loosely ch 7.

**Row 1:** Starting in 2nd ch from hook, sc 6, turn. (6 sts)

**Row 2:** Ch 1, sc 6, turn. (6 sts)

**Row 3:** Ch 1, sk 1, FPsc around the next 5 stitch posts, turn.

**Row 4:** Working in the tops of the 6 exposed sts of row 3 (directly in front of the FPsc sts), ch 1, sc 6, turn. (6 sts)

**Row 5:** Ch 1, sc 6, turn. (6 sts)

**Row 6:** Ch 1, sk 1, BPsc around the next 5 stitch posts, turn.

**Row 7:** Working in the tops of the 6 sts of row 6 (directly in back of the BPsc sts), ch 1, sc 6, turn. (6 sts)

Rep rows 2–7 9 more times until you have 20 ridges.

Sc along 1 long edge (this will become the outside edge of the track). Sl st along short edge and then along remaining long edge (this will become the inside edge of the track). Cut yarn and fasten off, leaving a long tail for sewing.

To complete the track and roller unit, sew the short edges of the track together to create a loop. With the sc edge facing out, slip the loop over the roller base.

With the roller detail facing out, sew the sl st edge to the back edge of the roller base.

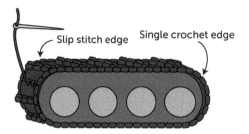

Slip stitch edge    Single crochet edge

With the slip stitch edge of the track against the side of the dark gray base, sew the side edges of the base to the back sides of the track roller bases.

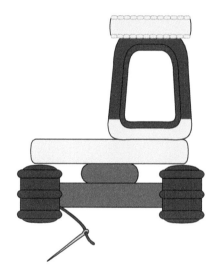

## AXLE PIN (MAKE 5)

In light gray, make a 6-st adjustable ring.

**Rnd 1:** In bl; sc 6. (6 sts)

**Rnd 2:** Sc2tog 3 times. (3 sts)

Cut yarn and fasten off, leaving a long tail for sewing.

Cinch hole closed with yarn tail. Thread the yarn tail back and forth through the center of the axle pin 3 to 4 times, pulling tightly as you sew to flatten the axle pin.

## BOOM

In yellow, loosely ch 31.

**Rnd 1:** Starting in 2nd ch and working in back ridge loops, sc 18, sc 3 in next st, sc 10, sc 4 in next ch. Rotate chain so front side of chain is facing up. Starting in front side of the next ch, sc 10, sc3tog, sc 15, sc 2 in front side of next ch. (63 sts)

**Rnd 2:** Dc 2 in next st, dc 6, hdc 11, sc 1, sc 3 in next st, sc 11, sc 2 in next 4 sts, sc 9, sc2tog, hdc 9, dc 6, dc 2 in next 2 sts. (71 sts)

**Rnd 3:** Bpsc 71. (71 sts)

**Rnds 4–5:** Sc 71. (71 sts)

**Rnd 6:** Bpsc 71. (71 sts)

**Rnd 7:** Dc2tog, dc 6, hdc 11, sc 1, sc3tog, sc 11, sc2tog 4 times, sc 9, sc 2 in next st, hdc 9, dc 6, dc2tog 2 times. (63 sts)

**Rnd 8:** Sc 18, sc3tog, sc 10, sc4tog, sc 10, sc 3 in next st, sc 15, sc2tog. (59 sts)

Cut yarn and fasten off, leaving a long tail for sewing.

### Boom tab (make 2)

The top of the boom is the thinner/tapered end. At the top of the boom on one side, locate the center surface stitch from rnd 3. Mark this stitch with a pm. Count 3 sts to the right of this st and pm. Remove the center pm.

**Row 1:** With yellow, begin by working in the pm surface stitch, (sl st, ch 1, sc 1). Cont working into the next 6 sts; hdc 1, dc 3, hdc 1, (sc 1, sl st 1) in next st, turn. (7 sts)

**Row 2:** Sk sl st, sc 2, sc 2 in next 3 sts, sc 2, turn. (10 sts)

**Row 3:** Ch 1, in bl; sc 10, turn. (10 sts)

**Row 4:** Ch 1, in fl; sc 2, sc2tog 3 times, sc 2. (7 sts)

Cut yarn and fasten off.

Rep on other side of boom.

Using 1-inch (25mm) cushion foam, cut (1) boom arm piece from template (page 113). Insert foam inside boom. Close up the seam in a straight line using a mattress stitch.

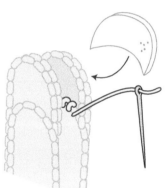

Using foam stabilizer, cut (2) boom tab pieces from template (page 113). Insert into the boom tab spaces and sew seams down to the top of the boom.

## EXCAVATOR BUCKET ARM

In yellow, loosely ch 19.

**Rnd 1:** Starting in 2nd ch and working in back ridge loops, sc 17, sc 4 in next ch. Rotate chain so front side of chain is facing up. Starting in front side of the next ch, sc 16, sc 2 in front side of next ch. (39 sts)

**Rnd 2:** Sc 2 in next st, sc 9, hdc 7, dc 2 in next 4 sts, hdc 7, sc 9, sc 2 in next 2 sts. (46 sts)

**Rnd 3:** Bpsc 46. (46 sts)

**Rnd 4:** Bpsc 46. (46 sts)

**Rnd 5:** Sc 46. (46 sts)

**Rnd 6:** Sc2tog, sc 9, hdc 7, dc2tog 4 times, hdc 7, sc 9, sc2tog 2 times. (39 sts)

Cut yarn and fasten off, leaving a long tail for sewing.

Using foam stabilizer, cut (1) excavator bucket arm piece from template (page 112). Place foam inside excavator bucket arm and sew seam closed in a straight line using a mattress stitch.

Place the larger end of the excavator bucket arm between the two boom tabs at the top of the boom. Draw the yarn tail of one axle pin through one side of the first boom tab, through the excavator arm, and through the opposite side of the 2nd boom tab. Pull firmly and fasten off. Starting on the opposite side of the 2nd boom tab, draw the yarn tail of the 2nd axle pin through the all the same openings as the first axle pin. Secure yarn under the first axle pin, pulling firmly to create a tight pivot.

Sew 2 more axle pins on thinner tapered end of the bucket arm.

## EXCAVATOR ARM BASE

With yellow, make an 8-st adjustable ring.

**Rnd 1:** Sc 2 in each st around. (16 sts)

**Rnd 2:** *Sc 1, sc 2 in next st; rep from * around. (24 sts)

**Rnd 3:** *Sc 2, sc 2 in next st; rep from * around. (32 sts)

**Rnd 4:** *Sc 3, sc 2 in next st; rep from * around. (40 sts)

**Rnd 5:** In bl; sc 20 and leave remaining 20 sts unworked. (20 sts)

Cut yarn and fasten off, leaving a long tail for sewing.

Using foam stabilizer, cut out (1) 3-inch (8cm) circle. Cut circle in half and place halves together. Fold excavator arm base in half so the sc 20 from rnd 5 is on one half. Insert doubled-up foam semi-circle; sew seams shut.

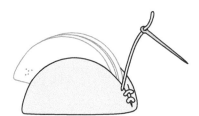

Sew the flat edge of the semi-circle crane arm base to the back half of the platform with 1 inch (25mm) of space between the base and the side of the rear engine.

Place one end of completed excavator arm in between excavator arm base and rear engine. Draw the light gray axle pin yarn tail through the excavator arm base and excavator arm, and catch the side of the rear engine. Draw yarn back out following the original path of the yarn through the excavator arm and excavator arm base. Bring yarn out through front of axle pin and pull very tightly to sandwich the excavator arm between the excavator arm base and rear engine. Secure yarn and sew in yarn tails.

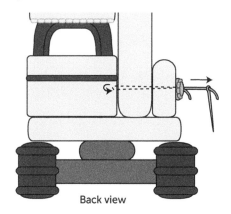

Back view

## EXCAVATOR BUCKET SIDE (MAKE 2)

With light gray, make an 8-st adjustable ring.

**Rnd 1:** Sc 2 in each st around. (16 sts)

**Rnd 2:** *Sc 1, sc 2 in next st; rep from * around. (24 sts)

**Rnd 3:** *Sc 2, sc 2 in next st; rep from * around. (32 sts)

**Rnd 4:** *Sc 7, sc 2 in next st; rep from * around. (36 sts)

**Rnd 5:** In bl; sc 18 and leave remaining 18 sts unworked. (18 sts)

# EXCAVATOR ////

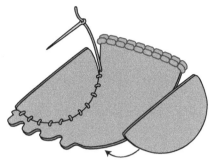

Using foam stabilizer, cut out (1) 4½ x 3¼-inch (11 x 8cm) rectangle and insert between the excavator bucket center layers. Sew up side seams with a whip stitch.

Match up the whip-stitched sides of the excavator bucket center with the rounded sides of the excavator bucket sides. Sew the edges of the excavator bucket center to the inside surface of the excavator bucket sides.

## EXCAVATOR BUCKET STRAP (MAKE 2)

In light gray, loosely ch 7.

Cut yarn and fasten off, leaving a long tail.

Attach the ends of the bucket straps to the top edge of the excavator bucket to the left and right of center with about 1 st of space between them to make 2 loops. Slide the loops over the 2 axle pins at the end of the excavator bucket arm. It should be a snug fit.

Cut yarn and fasten off, leaving a long tail for sewing.

Using foam stabilizer, cut out (1) 3-inch (8cm) circle. Cut circle in half. Fold excavator bucket side in half so the sc 18 from rnd 5 is on one half. Insert 1 foam semi-circle and sew seams shut. Rep on other side.

## EXCAVATOR BUCKET CENTER

With light gray, loosely ch 13.

**Row 1:** Starting in 2nd ch from hook, sc 12, turn. (12 sts)

**Rows 2–16:** Ch 1, sc 12, turn. (12 sts)

**Row 17:** Ch 1, in bl; sc 12, turn. (12 sts)

**Row 18:** Ch 1, in fl; sc 12, turn. (12 sts)

**Rows 19–32:** Ch 1, sc 12, turn. (12 sts)

**Row 33:** Fold piece in half and line up row 1 and row 32 with the surface loops of rows 17 and 18 facing out. Holding edges together, sc 12 with row 1 and row 33 tog, turn. (12 sts)

**Row 34:** *Sl st 1, (sl st 1, ch 2, hdc 2, ch 2, sl st 1) in next st, sl st 1; rep from * to end.

Cut yarn and fasten off, leaving a long tail for sewing.

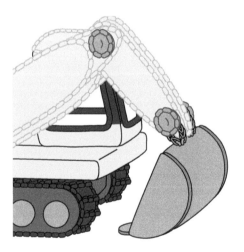

## AUGER

Starting with light gray, make an 8-st adjustable ring.

**Rnd 1:** Sc 2 in each st around. (16 sts)

**Rnd 2:** *Sc 1, sc 2 in next st; rep from * around. (24 sts)

**Rnd 3:** *Sc 2, sc 2 in next st; rep from * around. (32 sts)

**Rnds 4–5:** BPsc 32. (32 sts)

**Rnd 6:** *Sc 2, sc2tog; rep from * around. (24 sts)

Cut light gray. Change to dark gray.

Using foam stabilizer, cut out (1) 2½-inch (6cm) circle and insert into top of auger.

**Rnd 7:** FPsc 24. (24 sts)

**Rnd 8:** In bl; *hdc 4, hdc2tog; rep from * around. (20 sts)

**Rnd 9:** In bl; *hdc 3, hdc2tog; rep from * around. (16 sts)

**Rnd 10:** In bl; *hdc 2, hdc2tog; rep from * around. (12 sts)

**Rnd 11:** In bl; *hdc 1, hdc2tog; rep from * around. (8 sts)

Stuff auger.

**Rnd 12:** In bl; hdc2tog 4 times. (4 sts)

Cut yarn and fasten off, leaving a long tail for sewing.

**Auger drill detail**
Working in the surface loops of rnds 8–12, (sl st, ch 1) in surface loops of first st in rnd 8. Sl st in each surface loop from rnds 8–12. Cut yarn and fasten off, leaving a long tail for sewing.

## AUGER STRAP (MAKE 2)

In light gray, loosely ch 7.

Cut yarn and fasten off, leaving a long tail.

Attach the ends of the auger straps to the top edge of the auger to the left and right of center with about 1 st of space between them to make 2 loops. Slide the loops over the 2 axle pins at the end of the excavator bucket arm. It should be a snug fit.

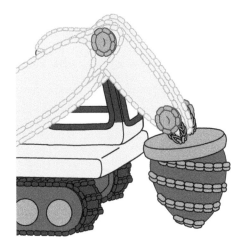

Weave in any remaining yarn tails.

# BULLDOZER

**FINISHED SIZE:** 10 x 8 x 8 in. (25 x 20 x 20cm) /// **YARN WEIGHT:**

Bulldozer loves to get down and dirty while building mighty ramps and pushing the biggest boulders about with the greatest of ease. With chunky tracks, a generous front blade, and extra-fun details like lift cylinders and a smokestack, this soft and squishy project is a must-have addition for any junior foreman or forewoman's worksite!

## MATERIALS & TOOLS

- Bulky yarn in black (150 yds/137m), dark gray (150 yds/137m), light gray (100 yds/91m), white (100 yds/91m), and yellow (300 yds/274m)
- Hook size I (5.5mm)
- Scissors
- Tapestry needle
- Polyester fiberfill
- 1-in. (25mm)-thick cushion foam
- Foam stabilizer

## INSTRUCTIONS

### CAB

Starting with yellow, loosely ch 8.

**Rnd 1:** Starting in 2nd ch and working in back ridge loops, sc 6, sc 4 in next ch. Rotate chain so front side of chain is facing up. Starting in front side of the next ch, sc 5, sc 3 in front side of next ch. (18 sts)

**Rnd 2:** Sc 3 in next st, sc 5, sc 3 in next st, sc 2, sc 3 in next st, sc 5, sc 3 in next st, sc 2. (26 sts)

**Rnd 3:** Sc 1, sc 3 in next st, sc 7, sc 3 in next st, sc 4, sc 3 in next st, sc 7, sc 3 in next st, sc 3. (34 sts)

**Rnd 4:** Sc 2, sc 3 in next st, sc 9, sc 3 in next st, sc 6, sc 3 in next st, sc 9, sc 3 in next st, sc 4. (42 sts)

**Rnd 5:** Sc 3, sc 3 in next st, sc 11, sc 3 in next st, sc 8, sc 3 in next st, sc 11, sc 3 in next st, sc 5. (50 sts)

# BULLDOZER ////

## Cab back wall

To begin: Sl st 5, turn.

**Row 1:** Ch 1, in fl; sc 10. Pm in next st. Turn work. (10 sts)

**Rows 2–3:** Ch 1, sc 10, turn. (10 sts)

Cut yellow. Change to black. Keep yarn tails on backside of work on row 4.

**Row 4:** Ch 1, sc 1, cut black, leaving a 48-inch (1.2m) tail to work with, change to white, sc 8, rejoin black from skein, sc 1, turn. (10 sts)

**Rows 5–8:** Ch 1, sc 1, change to white, sc 8, change to black, sc 1, turn. (10 sts)

**Row 9:** Ch 1, sc 1, change to white, sc2tog, sc 4, sc2tog, change to black, sc 1, turn. (8 sts)

**Rows 10–14:** Ch 1, sc 1, change to white, sc 6, change to black, sc 1, turn. (8 sts)

Cut white.

**Row 15:** Ch 1, sc2tog, sc 4, sc2tog, turn. (6 sts)

**Row 16:** Ch 1, sc 6, turn. (6 sts)

Cut yarn and fasten off, leaving a long tail for sewing.

## Side wall 1

**Row 1:** Starting with yellow, (sl st, ch 1, sc 1) in fl of pm stitch to re-attach yarn. Cont working in fl; sc 14. Pm in next st. Turn work. (15 sts)

**Rows 2–3:** Ch 1, sc 15, turn. (15 sts)

Change to black. Keep yarn tails on back side of work on row 4.

**Row 4:** Ch 1, sc 1, cut black, leaving a 48-inch (1.2m) tail to work with, change to yellow, sc 13, rejoin black from skein, sc 1, turn. (15 sts)

**Row 5:** Ch 1, sc 1, change to yellow, sc 13, change to black, sc 1, turn. (15 sts)

**Row 6:** Ch 1, sc 1, change to yellow, sc2tog, sc 11, change to black, sc 1, turn. (14 sts)

**Row 7:** Ch 1, sc 1, change to yellow, sc 12, change to black, sc 1, turn. (14 sts)

Cut yellow.

**Row 8:** Ch 1, sc 1, change to white, sc 12, change to black, sc 1, turn. (14 sts)

**Row 9:** Ch 1, sc 1, change to white, sc 10, sc2tog, change to black, sc 1, turn. (13 sts)

**Rows 10–11:** Ch 1, sc 1, change to white, sc 11, change to black, sc 1, turn. (13 sts)

**Row 12:** Ch 1, sc 1, change to white, sc2tog, sc 9, change to black, sc 1, turn. (12 sts)

**Rows 13–14:** Ch 1, sc 1, change to white, sc 10, change to black, sc 1, turn. (12 sts)

Cut white.

**Row 15:** Ch 1, sc 10, sc2tog, turn. (11 sts)

**Row 16:** Ch 1, sc 11, turn. (11 sts)

Cut yarn and fasten off, leaving a long tail for sewing.

## Front cab wall

**Row 1:** Starting with yellow, (sl st, ch 1, sc 1) in fl of pm stitch to re-attach yarn. Cont working in fl; sc 9. Pm in next st. Turn work. (10 sts)

Starting at row 2, rep back cab wall.

## Side wall 2

**Row 1:** Starting with yellow, (sl st, ch 1, sc 1) in fl of pm stitch to re-attach yarn. Cont working in fl; sc 14. Turn work. (15 sts)

**Rows 2–3:** Ch 1, sc 15, turn. (15 sts)

Change to black. Keep yarn tails on back side of work.

**Row 4:** Ch 1, sc 1, cut black, leaving a 48-inch (1.2m) tail to work with, change to yellow, sc 13, rejoin black from skein, sc 1, turn. (15 sts)

**Row 5:** Ch 1, sc 1, change to yellow, sc 13, change to black, sc 1, turn. (15 sts)

**Row 6:** Ch 1, sc 1, change to yellow, sc 11, sc2tog, change to black, sc 1, turn. (14 sts)

**Row 7:** Ch 1, sc 1, change to yellow, sc 12, change to black, sc 1, turn. (14 sts)

**Row 8:** Ch 1, sc 1, change to white, sc 12, change to black, sc 1, turn. (14 sts)

**Row 9:** Ch 1, sc 1, change to white, sc2tog, sc 10, change to black, sc 1, turn. (13 sts)

**Rows 10–11:** Ch 1, sc 1, change to white, sc 11, change to black, sc 1, turn. (13 sts)

**Row 12:** Ch 1, sc 1, change to white, sc 9, sc2tog, change to black, sc 1, turn. (12 sts)

**Rows 13–14:** Ch 1, sc 1, change to white, sc 10, change to black, sc 1, turn. (12 sts)

Cut white.

**Row 15:** Ch 1, sc2tog, sc 10, turn. (11 sts)

**Row 16:** Ch 1, sc 11, turn. (11 sts)

Cut yarn and fasten off, leaving a long tail for sewing.

Sew up side edges.

# BULLDOZER ////

## CAB ROOF

In yellow, loosely ch 6.

**Rnd 1:** Starting in 2nd ch and working in back ridge loops, sc 4, sc 4 in next ch. Rotate chain so front side of chain is facing up. Starting in front side of the next ch, sc 3, sc 3 in front side of next ch. (14 sts)

**Rnd 2:** Sc 3 in next st, sc 3, sc 3 in next st, sc 2, sc 3 in next st, sc 3, sc 3 in next st, sc 2. (22 sts)

**Rnd 3:** Sc 1, sc 3 in next st, sc 5, sc 3 in next st, sc 4, sc 3 in next st, sc 5, sc 3 in next st, sc 3. (30 sts)

**Rnd 4:** Sc 2, sc 3 in next st, sc 7, sc 3 in next st, sc 6, sc 3 in next st, sc 7, sc 3 in next st, sc 4. (38 sts)

**Rnd 5:** Sc 3, sc 3 in next st, sc 9, sc 3 in next st, sc 8, sc 3 in next st, sc 9, sc 3 in next st, sc 5. (46 sts)

**Rnd 6:** In bl; sc 46. (46 sts)

**Rnd 7:** In bl; sc 3, sc3tog, sc 9, sc3tog, sc 8, sc3tog, sc 9, sc3tog, sc 5. (38 sts)

**Rnd 8:** Sc 2, sc3tog, sc 7, sc3tog, sc 6, sc3tog, sc 7, sc3tog, sc 4. (30 sts)

**Rnd 9:** Sc 1, sc3tog, sc 5, sc3tog, sc 4, sc3tog, sc 5, sc3tog, sc 3. (22 sts)

Using foam stabilizer, cut out (1) 3¼ x 3-inch (8 x 8cm) rectangle. Insert foam into roof.

**Rnd 10:** Sc3tog, sc 3, sc3tog, sc 2, sc3tog, sc 3, sc3tog, sc 2. (14 sts)

**Rnd 11:** Sc 14. (14 sts)

Cut yarn and fasten off, leaving a long tail for sewing.

Sew the roof seam closed. With roof seam side down, sew bottom edge of roof to the open edge of the cab. Add more stuffing if needed before closing seam.

## CAB HOOD

Starting with yellow, loosely ch 8.

**Rnd 1:** Starting in 2nd ch and working in back ridge loops, sc 6, sc 4 in next ch. Rotate chain so front side of chain is facing up. Starting in front side of the next ch, sc 5, sc 3 in front side of next ch. (18 sts)

**Rnd 2:** Sc 3 in next st, sc 5, sc 3 in next st, sc 2, sc 3 in next st, sc 5, sc 3 in next st, sc 2. (26 sts)

**Rnd 3:** Sc 2 in next st, sc 3 in next st, sc 7, sc 3 in next st, sc 4, sc 3 in next st, sc 7, sc 3 in next st, sc 2 in next st, sc 2. (36 sts)

**Rnd 4:** Sc 3, sc 3 in next st, sc 9, sc 3 in next st, sc2tog, sc 2, sc2tog, sc 3 in next st, sc 9, sc 3 in next st, sc 5. (42 sts)

### Hood back wall
To begin: Sl st 4, turn.

**Row 1:** Ch 1, in fl; sc 10. Pm in next st. Turn work. (10 sts)

**Rows 2–6:** Ch 1, sc 10, turn. (10 sts)

**Row 7:** Ch 1, sc 10. (10 sts)

Cut yarn and fasten off, leaving a long tail for sewing.

### Hood side wall 1
**Row 1:** With yellow, (sl st, ch 1, sc 1) in fl of pm stitch to re-attach yarn. Cont working in fl; sc 11. Pm in next st. Turn work. (12 sts)

**Rows 2–3:** Ch 1, sc 12, turn. (12 sts)

**Row 4:** Ch 1, sc2tog, sc 10, turn. (11 sts)

**Row 5:** Ch 1, sc 11, turn. (11 sts)

**Row 6:** Ch 1, sc2tog, sc 9, turn. (10 sts)

**Row 7:** Ch 1, sc 5, sl st 5. (10 sts)

Cut yarn and fasten off, leaving a long tail for sewing.

### Hood front
**Row 1:** In yellow, (sl st, ch 1, sc 1) in fl of pm stitch to re-attach yarn. Cont working in fl; sc 7. Pm in next st. Turn work. (8 sts)

**Rows 2–3:** Ch 1, sc 8, turn. (8 sts)

**Row 4:** Ch 1, sc2tog, sc 4, sc2tog, turn. (6 sts)

**Row 5:** Ch 1, sc 6, turn. (6 sts)

**Row 6:** Ch 1, sc 2, sc2tog, sc 2, turn. (5 sts)

**Row 7:** Ch 1, sc 5, turn. (5 sts)

**Row 8:** Ch 1, bl; sc 5, turn. (5 sts)

**Rows 9–10:** Ch 1, sc 5, turn. (5 sts)

**Row 11:** Ch 1, sc 2, sc 2 in next st, sc 2, turn. (6 sts)

**Rows 12–13:** Ch 1, sc 6, turn. (6 sts)

**Row 14:** Ch 1, sc 2 in next st, sc 4, sc 2 in next st. (8 sts)

**Rows 15–16:** Ch 1, sc 8, turn. (8 sts)

**Row 17:** Ch 1, sc 2 in next st, sc 6, sc 2 in next st. (10 sts)

Cut yarn and fasten off, leaving a long tail for sewing.

**Hood side wall 2**
**Row 1:** With yellow, (sl st, ch 1, sc 1) in fl of pm stitch to re-attach yarn. Cont working in fl; sc 11. Turn work. (12 sts)

**Rows 2–3:** Ch 1, sc 12, turn. (12 sts)

**Row 4:** Ch 1, sc 10, sc2tog, turn. (11 sts)

**Row 5:** Ch 1, sc 11, turn. (11 sts)

**Row 6:** Ch 1, sc 9, sc2tog, turn. (10 sts)

**Row 7:** Ch 1, sl st 5, sc 5. (10 sts)

Cut yarn and fasten off, leaving a long tail for sewing.

Sew edges together with a whip stitch and stuff before closing seam. Line up the bottom of the pieces and sew the back hood wall to the front of the cab.

## GRILL

Using black, loosely ch 9.

**Row 1:** Starting in 2nd chain from hook, sc 8, turn. (8 sts)

**Row 2:** Ch 1, sl st 8 loosely, turn. (8 sts)

**Row 3:** Ch 1, sc 8, turn. (8 sts)

**Row 4:** Ch 1, sl st 8 loosely, turn. (8 sts)

**Row 5:** Ch 1, sc2tog, sc 4, sc2tog, turn. (6 sts)

**Row 6:** Ch 1, sl st 6 loosely, turn. (6 sts)

**Row 7:** Ch 1, sc 2, sc2tog, sc 2, turn. (5 sts)

**Row 8:** Ch 1, sl st 5 loosely, turn. (5 sts)

Sl st around outside edges of the grill until you have reached the other side of row 8.

Cut yarn and fasten off, leaving a long tail for sewing.

Sew the grill onto the front of the hood.

## BULLDOZER BASE

Using yellow, loosely ch 59.

**Row 1:** Starting in 2nd ch from hook, sc 58, turn. (58 sts)

**Rows 2–3:** Ch 1, sc 58, turn. (58 sts)

Cut yarn and fasten off, leaving a long tail for sewing. Turn work.

**Row 4:** Count 25 sts in from end. Working in fl of 25th st, (sl st 1, ch 1, sc 1). Cont to work down the row in fl; sc 9, turn. (10 sts)

**Rows 5–29:** Ch 1, sc 10, turn. (10 sts)

**Row 30:** Ch 1, in fl; sc 10, turn. (10 sts)

**Rows 31–32:** Ch 1, sc 10, turn. (10 sts)

**Row 33:** Ch 1, in bl; sc 10, turn. (10 sts)

**Rows 34–57:** Ch 1, sc 10, turn. (10 sts)

Cut yarn and fasten off, leaving a long tail for sewing.

With the surface loops of the bulldozer base facing out, sew row 57 to the middle of row 1.

Using 1-in.-thick cushion foam, cut out (1) 2¾ x 7-inch (7 x 18cm) rectangle. Insert foam pieces between the top and bottom layers of the base. Pin side edges in place and sew edges together with a whip stitch.

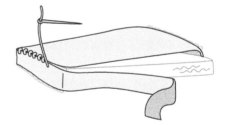

Sew the cab and hood to the bulldozer base.

Double up black yarn on a tapestry needle and embroider a chain stitch around each window as well as some window pane details (refer to photos for reference).

# BULLDOZER ////

## SMOKESTACK

With black, make a 4-st adjustable ring.

**Rnd 1:** In bl; sc 4. (4 sts)

**Rnds 2–4:** Sc 4. (4 sts)

**Smokestack flap**
In fl of next st, (sl st 1, ch 2, hdc 2, ch 2, sl st 1).

Cut yarn and fasten off, leaving a long tail for sewing.

Sew bottom of smokestack to top of hood.

## ROLLER BASE (MAKE 2)

With dark gray, loosely ch 16.

**Rnd 1:** Starting in 2nd ch and working in back ridge loops, sc 14, sc 4 in next ch. Rotate chain so front side of chain is facing up. Starting in front side of the next ch, sc 13, sc 3 in front side of next ch. (34 sts)

**Rnd 2:** Sc 2 in next st, sc 13, sc 2 in next 4 sts, sc 13, sc 2 in next 3 sts. (42 sts)

**Rnd 3:** Sc 2 in next st, sc 17, sc 2 in next 4 sts, sc 17, sc 2 in next 3 sts. (50 sts)

**Rnd 4:** In bl; sc 50. (50 sts)

**Rnds 5–6:** Sc 50. (50 sts)

**Rnd 7:** In bl; sc2tog, sc 17, sc2tog 4 times, sc 17, sc2tog 3 times. (42 sts)

**Rnd 8:** Sc2tog, sc 13, sc2tog 4 times, sc 13, sc2tog 3 times. (34 sts)

**Rnd 9:** Sc 34. (34 sts)

Cut yarn and fasten off, leaving a long tail. Stuff and close seam.

## FINAL DRIVE BASE (MAKE 2)

With dark gray, make a 6-st adjustable ring.

**Rnd 1:** Sc 2 in each st around. (12 sts)

**Rnd 2:** *Sc 1, sc 2 in next st; rep from * 5 more times. (18 sts)

**Rnd 3:** In bl; sc 18. (18 sts)

**Rnds 4–5:** Sc 18. (18 sts)

**Rnd 6:** In bl; *sc 1, sc2tog; rep from * 5 more times. (12 sts)

Stuff.

**Rnd 7:** Sc2tog 6 times. (6 sts)

Cut yarn and fasten off, leaving a long tail for sewing. Close hole in back of final drive base.

## ROLLER (MAKE 8)

With light gray, make a 4-st adjustable ring.

**Rnd 1:** Sc 2 in each st around. (8 sts)

Cut yarn and fasten off, leaving a long tail for sewing.

Sew 4 rollers to the front of the roller base along the bottom edge. Rep on other base.

## FINAL DRIVE (MAKE 2)

With light gray, make a 4-st adjustable ring.

**Rnd 1:** Sc 2 in each st around. (8 sts)

**Rnd 2:** *Sc 1, sc 2 in next st; rep from * 3 more times. (12 sts)

Cut yarn and fasten off, leaving a long tail for sewing.

Sew final drive onto the front of the final drive base. Rep on other base.

With one roller base lying horizontal, sew the side of the one final drive base to the top side of the roller base close to the right edge. Rep on other roller base but place final drive base close to left edge.

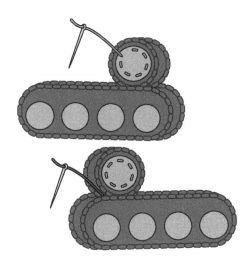

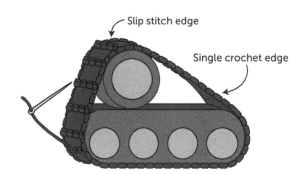

Slip stitch edge

Single crochet edge

With the sl st edge of the track against the side of the cab, sew the track roller unit in place. The middle of the roller base will line up with the bottom edge of the cab base and the final drive will line up under the cab side window.

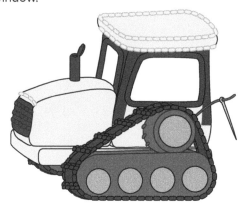

## TRACK (MAKE 2)

In black, loosely ch 7, turn.

**Row 1:** Starting in 2nd ch from hook, sc 6, turn. (6 sts)

**Row 2:** Ch 1, sc 6, turn. (6 sts)

**Row 3:** Ch 1, sk 1, FPsc 5 around the 5 available st posts, turn.

**Row 4:** Working in the tops of the 6 exposed sts of row 3 (directly in front of the FPsc sts), ch 1, sc 6, turn. (6 sts)

**Row 5:** Ch 1, sc 6, turn. (6 sts)

**Row 6:** Ch 1, sk 1, BPsc 5 around the 5 available st posts, turn.

**Row 7:** Working in the tops of the 6 sts of row 6 (directly in back of the BPsc sts), ch 1, sc 6, turn. (6 sts)

Rep rows 2–7 9 more times until you have 20 ridges.

Sc along 1 long edge (this will become the outside edge of the track). Sl st along short edge and then along remaining long edge (this will become the inside edge of the track). Cut yarn and fasten off, leaving a long tail for sewing.

To complete the track and roller unit, sew the short ends of the track together to create a loop. With the sc edge facing out, slip the loop over the final drive/roller base and tack in place with a few sts where the track touches the roller base and final drive.

## BLADE CENTER

In yellow, loosely ch 21, turn.

**Row 1:** Starting in 2nd ch from hook and working in back ridge loops, sc 20, turn. (20 sts)

**Rows 2–13:** Ch 1, sc 20, turn. (20 sts)

**Row 14:** Ch 1, fl; sc 20, turn. (20 sts)

**Row 15:** Ch 1, bl; sc 20, turn. (20 sts)

**Rows 16–26:** Ch 1, sc 20, turn. (20 sts)

Cut yarn and fasten off, leaving a long tail for sewing.

### Blade sides

Fold blade over and match up row 1 and row 26 with surface loops on rows 14 and 15, facing out.

**Row 1:** Working through the front and back of blade at the same time, (sl st 1, ch 1, sc 1) at a corner at the bottom edge of the blade (counts as first sc). Cont to sc 11 more sts along the side edge, turn. (12 sts)

**Row 2:** Ch 1, sc 6, hdc 6, turn. (12 sts)

**Row 3:** Ch 1, hdc 6, sc 6, turn. (12 sts)

# BULLDOZER ////

**Row 4:** Ch 1, sc 12.

Cut yarn and fasten off, leaving a long tail for sewing. Fold edge over towards the blade. Sew row 4 to row 1. Rep on other side.

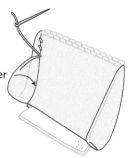

Fold over

Using foam stabilizer, cut out (1) 5½ x 3-inch (14 x 8cm) rectangle and insert into blade.

## Blade bottom

Working through the front and back edges of the bottom of the blade at the same time, (sl st 1, ch 1, sc 1) at the corner of the opening. Cont to sc along bottom edge until you reach the end, turn. *Ch 1 and sc to end. Turn. Rep from * 1 more time. Cut yarn and fasten off, leaving a long tail for sewing.

Sew the side edges of the blade bottom to the bottom edges of the blade sides.

## PUSH FRAME (MAKE 2)

In yellow, loosely ch 19, turn.

**Row 1:** Starting in 2nd ch from hook and working in back ridge loops, sc 18, turn. (18 sts)

**Rows 2–3:** Ch 1, sc 18, turn. (18 sts)

**Row 4:** Ch 1, fl; sc 18, turn. (18 sts)

**Row 5:** Ch 1, bl; sc 18, turn. (18 sts)

**Rows 6–7:** Ch 1, sc 18, turn. (18 sts)

Cut yarn and fasten off, leaving a long tail for sewing.

Using foam stabilizer, cut out (2) 5 x ¾-inch (13 x 2cm) strips. Fold push frame the long way with rows 1 and 7 together and surface loops of rows 4 and 5 facing out. Place foam inside and sew edges together.

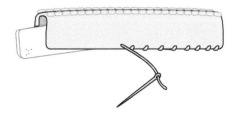

Sew one short end of each push frame to the back of the blade behind the middle of the side edges. Sew the side of the push frames to the front of the roller bases.

## LIFT CYLINDER (MAKE 2)

Starting with yellow, make an 8-st adjustable ring.

**Rnd 1:** In bl; sc 8. (8 sts)

**Rnds 2–5:** Sc 8. (8 sts)

Change to light gray. Stuff top of cylinder.

**Rnd 6:** In bl; sc2tog 4 times. (4 sts)

**Rnds 7–10*:** Sc 4. (4 sts)

(*feel free to make this longer if needed)

Cut yarn and fasten off, leaving a long tail for sewing.

Use a pencil or the handle of a smaller crochet hook to stuff the gray section of the piston.

Sew yellow part of pistons to the front side corners of the hood. Attach the end of the gray section to the back of the blade.

Weave in any remaining yarn tails.

# FORKLIFT

**FINISHED SIZE:** 8 x 6 x 8 in. (20 x 15 x 20cm)　///　**YARN WEIGHT:**

Small but mighty, this adorable forklift pattern includes a working set of forks and warning light and is sure to be a big hit on the construction site.

## MATERIALS & TOOLS

- Bulky-weight yarn in black (150 yds/137m), blue (20 yds/18m), dark gray (100 yds/91m), light gray (100 yds/91m), orange (150 yds/137m), and white (100 yds/91m)
- Hook size I (5.5mm)
- Scissors
- Tapestry needle
- Polyester fiberfill
- 1-in. (25mm)-thick cushion foam
- Foam stabilizer

## INSTRUCTIONS

### CAB

Starting with dark gray, loosely ch 6.

**Rnd 1:** Starting in 2nd ch and working in back ridge loops, sc 4, sc 4 in next ch. Rotate chain so front side of chain is facing up. Starting in front side of the next ch, sc 3, sc 3 in front side of next ch. (14 sts)

**Rnd 2:** Sc 3 in next st, sc 3, sc 3 in next st, sc 2, sc 3 in next st, sc 3, sc 3 in next st, sc 2. (22 sts)

**Rnd 3:** Sc 1, sc 3 in next st, sc 5, sc 3 in next st, sc 4, sc 3 in next st, sc 5, sc 3 in next st, sc 3. (30 sts)

**Rnd 4:** Sc 2, sc 3 in next st, sc 7, sc 3 in next st, sc 6, sc 3 in next st, sc 7, sc 3 in next st, sc 4. (38 sts)

**Rnd 5:** Sc 3, sc 3 in next st, sc 9, sc 3 in next st, sc 8, sc 3 in next st, sc 9, sc 3 in next st, sc 5. (46 sts)

## Cab back wall

To begin: Sl st 5, turn.

**Row 1:** Ch 1, in fl; sc 10. Pm in next st. Turn work. (10 sts)

**Row 2:** Ch 1, sc 10, turn. (10 sts)

Change to orange.

**Rows 3–6:** Ch 1, sc 10, turn. (10 sts)

Cut orange. Change to black. Keep yarn tails on front side of work for row 7.

**Row 7:** With 1 strand of black, ch 1, sc 1, change to white, sc 8, change to 2nd strand of black, sc 1, turn. (10 sts)

**Row 8:** Ch 1, sc 1, change to white, sc 8, change to black, sc 1, turn. (10 sts)

**Row 9:** Ch 1, sc 1, change to white, sc2tog, sc 4, sc2tog, change to black, sc 1, turn. (8 sts)

**Rows 10–14:** Ch 1, sc 1, change to white, sc 6, change to black, sc 1, turn. (8 sts)

Cut white.

**Row 15:** Ch 1, sc2tog, sc 4, sc2tog, turn. (6 sts)

**Row 16:** Ch 1, sc 6, turn. (6 sts)

Cut yarn and fasten off, leaving a long tail for sewing.

## Side wall 1

**Row 1:** Starting with dark gray, (sl st, ch 1, sc 1) in fl of pm stitch to re-attach yarn. Cont working in fl; sc 12. Pm in next st. Turn work. (13 sts)

**Row 2:** Ch 1, sc 13, turn. (13 sts)

Change to orange.

**Rows 3–5:** Ch 1, sc 13, turn. (13 sts)

Cut orange. Change to black. Keep yarn tails on the backside of your work for row 6.

**Row 6:** Ch 1, sc 1, cut black, leaving a 48-inch (1.2m) tail to work with, change to white, sc2tog, sc 9, rejoin black from skein, sc 1, turn. (12 sts)

**Rows 7–8:** Ch 1, sc 1, change to white, sc 10, change to black, sc 1, turn. (12 sts)

**Row 9:** Ch 1, sc 1, change to white, sc 8, sc2tog, change to black, sc 1, turn. (11 sts)

**Rows 10–11:** Ch 1, sc 1, change to white, sc 9, change to black, sc 1, turn. (11 sts)

**Row 12:** Ch 1, sc 1, change to white, sc2tog, sc 7 change to black, sc 1, turn. (10 sts)

**Rows 13–14:** Ch 1, sc 1, change to white, sc 8, change to black, sc 1, turn. (10 sts)

Cut white.

**Row 15:** Ch 1, sc 8, sc2tog, turn. (9 sts)

**Row 16:** Ch 1, sc 9, turn. (9 sts)

Cut yarn and fasten off, leaving a long tail for sewing.

## Front cab wall

**Row 1:** Starting with dark gray, (sl st, ch 1, sc 1) in fl of pm stitch to re-attach yarn. Cont working in fl; sc 9. Pm in next st. Turn work. (10 sts)

Rep cab back wall starting at row 2.

## Side wall 2

**Row 1:** Starting with dark gray, (sl st, ch 1, sc 1) in fl of pm stitch to re-attach yarn. Cont working in fl; sc 12. Turn work. (13 sts)

**Row 2:** Ch 1, sc 13, turn. (13 sts)

Change to orange.

**Rows 3–5:** Ch 1, sc 13, turn. (13 sts)

Cut orange. Change to black. Keep yarn tails on the backside of your work for row 6.

# FORKLIFT ////

**Row 6:** Ch 1, sc 1, cut black, leaving a 48-inch (1.2m) tail to work with, change to white, sc 9, sc2tog, rejoin black from skein, sc 1, turn. (12 sts)

**Rows 7–8:** Ch 1, sc 1, change to white, sc 10, change to black, sc 1, turn. (12 sts)

**Row 9:** Ch 1, sc 1, change to white, sc2tog, sc 8, change to black, sc 1, turn. (11 sts)

**Rows 10–11:** Ch 1, sc 1, change to white, sc 9, change to black, sc 1, turn. (11 sts)

**Row 12:** Ch 1, sc 1, change to white, sc 7, sc2tog, change to black, sc 1, turn. (10 sts)

**Rows 13–14:** Ch 1, sc 1, change to white, sc 8, change to black, sc 1, turn. (10 sts)

Cut white.

**Row 15:** Ch 1, sc2tog, sc 8, turn. (9 sts)

**Row 16:** Ch 1, sc 9, turn. (9 sts)

Cut yarn and fasten off, leaving a long tail for sewing.

Sew up side edges.

With 1-inch (25mm)-thick cushion foam, cut out (1) 4½ x 3-inch (11 x 8cm) rectangle and place at bottom of cab. Stuff the rest of the cab with fiberfill.

## CAB ROOF

In black, loosely ch 6.

**Rnd 1:** Starting in 2nd ch and working in back ridge loops, sc 4, sc 4 in next ch. Rotate chain so front side of chain is facing up. Starting in front side of the next ch, sc 3, sc 3 in front side of next ch. (14 sts)

**Rnd 2:** Sc 3 in next st, sc 3, sc 3 in next st, sc 2, sc 3 in next st, sc 3, sc 3 in next st, sc 2. (22 sts)

**Rnd 3:** Sc 1, sc 3 in next st, sc 5, sc 3 in next st, sc 4, sc 3 in next st, sc 5, sc 3 in next st, sc 3. (30 sts)

**Rnd 4:** Sc 2, sc 3 in next st, sc 7, sc 3 in next st, sc 6, sc 3 in next st, sc 7, sc 3 in next st, sc 4. (38 sts)

**Rnd 5:** Sc 3, sc 3 in next st, sc 9, sc 3 in next st, sc 8, sc 3 in next st, sc 9, sc 3 in next st, sc 5. (46 sts)

**Rnd 6:** In bl; sc 46. (46 sts)

**Rnd 7:** In bl; sc 3, sc3tog, sc 9, sc3tog, sc 8, sc3tog, sc 9, sc3tog, sc 5. (38 sts)

**Rnd 8:** Sc 2, sc3tog, sc 7, sc3tog, sc 6, sc3tog, sc 7, sc3tog, sc 4. (30 sts)

**Rnd 9:** Sc 1, sc3tog, sc 5, sc3tog, sc 4, sc3tog, sc 5, sc3tog, sc 3. (22 sts)

Using foam stabilizer, cut out (1) 3¼ x 3-inch (8 x 8cm) rectangle. Insert foam into roof.

**Rnd 10:** Sc3tog, sc 3, sc3tog, sc 2, sc3tog, sc 3, sc3tog, sc 2. (14 sts)

**Rnd 11:** Sc 14. (14 sts)

Cut yarn and fasten off, leaving a long tail for sewing.

Sew the roof seam closed. With roof seam side down, sew bottom edge of roof to the open edge of the cab. Add more stuffing if needed before closing seam.

Double up black yarn on a tapestry needle and embroider a chain stitch around each window (refer to photos for reference).

## WARNING LIGHT

Starting with blue, make a 4-st adjustable ring.

**Rnd 1:** In bl; sc 2 in each st around. (8 sts)

**Rnd 2:** Sc 8. (8 sts)

Cut blue. Change to light gray.

**Rnd 3:** In fl; *sc 1, sc 2 in each st around; rep from * 3 more times. (12 sts)

**Rnd 4:** In bl; sl st 12. (12 sts)

Cut yarn and fasten off, leaving a long tail for sewing.

Stuff and sew light to top of cab roof.

## FRONT TIRE (MAKE 2)

Using black, make a 6-st adjustable ring.

**Rnd 1:** Sc 2 in each st around. (12 sts)

**Rnd 2:** *Sc 1, sc 2 in next st; rep from * 5 more times. (18 sts)

**Rnd 3:** *Sc 2, sc 2 in next st; rep from * 5 more times. (24 sts)

**Rnds 4–5:** Sc 24. (24 sts)

**Rnd 6:** *Sc 2, sc2tog; rep from * 5 more times. (18 sts)

**Rnd 7:** *Sc 1, sc2tog; rep from * 5 more times. (12 sts)

Stuff tire.

**Rnd 8:** Sc2tog 6 times. (6 sts)

Fasten off yarn, leaving a long tail for sewing. Close the 6-st hole.

Thread the yarn tail back and forth through the center of the tire 3 to 4 times, pulling tightly as you sew to shape the tire.

## FRONT TIRE HUBCAP (MAKE 2)

Using light gray, make a 6-st adjustable ring.

**Rnd 1:** Sc 2 in each st around. (12 sts)

Cut yarn and fasten off, leaving a long tail for sewing.

Sew hubcaps to the sides of the tires.

## FRONT TIRE FENDER (MAKE 2)

Using orange, make a 5-st adjustable ring.

**Rnd 1:** Sc 2 in each st around. (10 sts)

**Rnds 2–15:** Sc 10. (10 sts)

**Rnd 16:** Sc2tog 5 times. (5 sts)

Fasten off yarn, leaving a long tail for sewing.

## BACK TIRE (MAKE 2)

Using black, make a 6-st adjustable ring.

**Rnd 1:** Sc 2 in each st around. (12 sts)

**Rnd 2:** *Sc 1, sc 2 in next st; rep from * 5 more times. (18 sts)

**Rnds 3–4:** Sc 18. (18 sts)

**Rnd 5:** *Sc 1, sc2tog; rep from * 5 more times. (12 sts)

Stuff tire.

**Rnd 6:** Sc2tog 6 times. (6 sts)

Fasten off yarn, leaving a long tail for sewing. Close the 6-st hole.

Thread the yarn tail back and forth through the center of the tire 3 to 4 times, pulling tightly as you sew to shape the tire.

## BACK TIRE HUBCAP (MAKE 2)

Using light gray, make a 4-st adjustable ring.

**Rnd 1:** Sc 2 in each st around. (8 sts)

Cut yarn and fasten off, leaving a long tail for sewing.

Sew hubcaps to the sides of the tires.

## BACK TIRE FENDER (MAKE 2)

Using orange, make a 5-st adjustable ring.

**Rnd 1:** Sc 2 in each st around. (10 sts)

**Rnds 2–12:** Sc 10. (10 sts)

**Rnd 13:** Sc2tog 5 times. (5 sts)

Fasten off yarn, leaving a long tail for sewing.

Wrap the corresponding fenders over the tops of the front and back tires and secure to the sides and top of the tire with a few stitches. Sew tires onto the sides of the cab, then sew the inside edge of the fender to the side of the cab.

## FORKS

In light gray, ch 11.

**Row 1:** Starting in 2nd ch from hook, sc 10, turn. (10 sts)

**Rows 2–5:** Ch 1, sc 10, turn. (10 sts)

**Row 6:** Ch 1, fl; sc 10, turn. (10 sts)

**Row 7:** Ch 1, bl; sc 1, ch 2, sk 2, sc 4, ch 2, sk 2, sc 1, turn. (10 sts)

**Row 8:** Ch 1, sc 1, sc 2 in ch-2 sp, sc 4, sc 2 in ch-2 sp, sc 1, turn. (10 sts)

**Rows 9–11:** Ch 1, sc 10, turn. (10 sts)

Fold piece so surface loops from rows 6 and 7 are facing out. Hold rows 1 and 11 tog and sl st 10 through both sets of sts. Cut yarn and fasten off, leaving a long tail for sewing.

### Fork arm (make 2)

**Rnd 1:** (Sl st 1, ch 1, sc 1) along the inside of edge of one of the ch-2 sps (counts as first st). Cont to sc around inside edge of ch-2 sp for 5 more sts. (6 sts)

**Rnds 2–7:** Sc 6. (6 sts)

Cut yarn and fasten off, leaving end opened.

Rep on other ch-2 sp.

Using foam stabilizer, cut out (1) 1¾ x 2¾-inch (4 x 7cm) rectangle and slide it into the side of the fork. Using foam stabilizer, cut out (2) 2 x ¾-inch (5 x 2cm) rectangles of purse foam. Insert foam into fork arms.

## FORK STRAP

In light gray, ch 11.

**Row 1:** Starting in 2nd ch from hook, sc 10, turn. (10 sts)

**Rows 2–3:** Ch 1, sc 10, turn. (10 sts)

Cut yarn and fasten off, leaving a long tail for sewing.

Attach strap horizontally across back of fork.

## FORK COLUMN

In dark gray, loosely ch 12. Sl st in first ch to make a loop, taking care not to twist the chain.

**Rnd 1:** Working in back ridge loops of ch-12, sc 12. (12 sts)

**Rnds 2–3:** Sc 12. (12 sts)

**Rnd 4:** In bl; sc 12. (12 sts)

**Rnds 5–18:** Sc 12. (12 sts)

**Rnd 19:** In bl; sc 12. (12 sts)

**Rnds 20–21:** Sc 12. (12 sts)

Cut yarn and fasten off, leaving a long tail for sewing.

Using foam stabilizer, cut out (1) 1¼ x 4-inch (3 x 10cm) rectangle. Insert foam between rnds 4 and 19. Flatten column and sew through rnd 4 and rnd 19 with a running stitch to secure the foam in the middle.

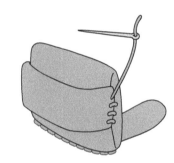

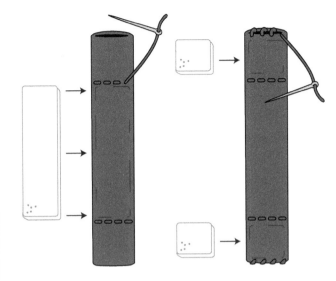

Using foam stabilizer, cut out (2) 1¼ x ¾-inch (3 x 2cm) rectangles. Insert into the ends of the column. Flatten ends and sew shut with a whip stitch.

Slide the fork onto the column. Sew the column ends onto the dark gray part of the cab and the black part above the front window. If the strap needs tightening, apply a few stitches between the fork and the fork strap on either side of the column, taking care not to sew through the fork column. Apply a whip stitch along the folded points in the column to create a crisper edge.

Weave in any remaining yarn tails.

# SKIDSTEER

**FINISHED SIZE:** 10 x 6 x 5½ in. (25 x 15 x 14cm)  **YARN WEIGHT:**

Skidsteer is ready to help out with small jobs on the worksite with its working bucket and zippy little wheels! Nothing would make it happier than a big pile of rocks to play with (page 110).

## MATERIALS & TOOLS

- Bulky-weight yarn in black (150 yds/137m), dark gray (100 yds/91m), light gray (100 yds/91m), white (100 yds/91m), and yellow (150 yds/137m)
- Hook size I (5.5mm)
- Place marker
- Scissors
- Tapestry needle
- Polyester fiberfill
- 1-in. (25mm)-thick cushion foam
- Foam stabilizer

## INSTRUCTIONS

### CAB

Starting with yellow, loosely ch 6.

**Rnd 1:** Starting in 2nd ch and working in back ridge loops, sc 4, sc 4 in next ch. Rotate chain so front side of chain is facing up. Starting in front side of the next ch, sc 3, sc 3 in front side of next ch. (14 sts)

**Rnd 2:** Sc 3 in next st, sc 3, sc 3 in next st, sc 2, sc 3 in next st, sc 3, sc 3 in next st, sc 2. (22 sts)

**Rnd 3:** Sc 1, sc 3 in next st, sc 5, sc 3 in next st, sc 4, sc 3 in next st, sc 5, sc 3 in next st, sc 3. (30 sts)

**Rnd 4:** Sc 2, sc 3 in next st, sc 7, sc 3 in next st, sc 6, sc 3 in next st, sc 7, sc 3 in next st, sc 4. (38 sts)

**Rnd 5:** Sc 3, sc 3 in next st, sc 9, sc 3 in next st, sc 8, sc 3 in next st, sc 9, sc 3 in next st, sc 5. (46 sts)

## Cab back wall

To begin: Sl st 5, turn.

**Row 1:** Ch 1, in fl; sc 10. Pm in next st. Turn work. (10 sts)

**Rows 2–8:** Ch 1, sc 10, turn. (10 sts)

Cut yellow, change to black. Keep yarn tails on side of work facing you for row 9.

**Row 9:** Ch 1, sc 1, cut black, leaving a 36-inch (.9m) tail to work with, change to white, sc2tog, sc 4, sc2tog, rejoin black from skein, sc 1, turn. (8 sts)

**Rows 10–14:** Ch 1, sc 1, change to white, sc 6, change to black, sc 1, turn. (8 sts)

Cut white.

**Row 15:** Ch 1, sc2tog, sc 4, sc2tog, turn. (6 sts)

**Row 16:** Ch 1, sc 6, turn. (6 sts)

Cut yarn and fasten off, leaving a long tail for sewing.

## Side wall 1

**Row 1:** Starting with yellow, (sl st, ch 1, sc 1) in fl of pm stitch to re-attach yarn. Cont working in fl; sc 12. Pm in

next st. Turn work. (13 sts)

**Rows 2–5:** Ch 1, sc 13, turn. (13 sts)

Cut yellow. Change to black. Keep yarn tails at the back of your work for row 6.

**Row 6:** Ch 1, sc 1, cut black, leaving a 48-inch (1.2m) tail to work with, change to white, sc2tog, sc 9, rejoin black from skein, sc 1, turn. (12 sts)

**Rows 7–8:** Ch 1, sc 1, change to white, sc 10, change to black, sc 1, turn. (12 sts)

**Row 9:** Ch 1, sc 1, change to white, sc 8, sc2tog, change to black, sc 1, turn. (11 sts)

**Rows 10–11:** Ch 1, sc 1, change to white, sc 9, change to black, sc 1, turn. (11 sts)

**Row 12:** Ch 1, sc 1, change to white, sc2tog, sc 7, change to black, sc 1, turn. (10 sts)

**Rows 13–14:** Ch 1, sc 1, change to white, sc 8, change to black, sc 1, turn. (10 sts)

Cut white.

**Row 15:** Ch 1, sc 8, sc2tog, turn. (9 sts)

**Row 16:** Ch 1, sc 9, turn. (9 sts)

Cut yarn and fasten off, leaving a long tail for sewing.

## Front cab wall

**Row 1:** Ch 1, in fl; sc 10. Pm in next st. Turn work. (10 sts)

**Rows 2–6:** Ch 1, sc 10, turn. (10 sts)

Cut yellow. Change to black. Keep yarn tails on front side of work for row 7.

**Row 7:** Ch 1, sc 1, cut black, leaving a 48-inch (1.2m) tail to work with, change to white, sc 8, rejoin black from skein, sc 1, turn. (10 sts)

**Row 8:** Ch 1, sc 1, change to white, sc 8, change to black, sc 1, turn. (10 sts)

**Row 9:** Ch 1, sc 1, change to white, sc2tog, sc 4, sc2tog, change to black, sc 1, turn. (8 sts)

Rep cab back wall starting at row 10.

## Side wall 2

**Row 1:** Starting with yellow, (sl st, ch 1, sc 1) in fl of pm stitch to re-attach yarn. Cont working in fl; sc 12. Turn work. (13 sts)

**Rows 2–5:** Ch 1, sc 13, turn. (13 sts)

Cut yellow. Change to black. Keep yarn tails at the back of your work for row 6.

**Row 6:** Ch 1, sc 1, cut black, leaving a 48-inch (1.2m) tail to work with, change to white, sc 9, sc2tog, rejoin black from skein, sc 1, turn. (12 sts)

**Rows 7–8:** Ch 1, sc 1, change to white, sc 10, change to black, sc 1, turn. (12 sts)

**Row 9:** Ch 1, sc 1, change to white, sc2tog, sc 8, change to black, sc 1, turn. (11 sts)

**Rows 10–11:** Ch 1, sc 1, change to white, sc 9, change to black, sc 1, turn. (11 sts)

**Row 12:** Ch 1, sc 1, change to white, sc 7, sc2tog, change to black, sc 1, turn. (10 sts)

**Rows 13–14:** Ch 1, sc 1, change to white, sc 8, change to black, sc 1, turn. (10 sts)

Cut white.

**Row 15:** Ch 1, sc2tog, sc 8, turn. (9 sts)

**Row 16:** Ch 1, sc 9, turn. (9 sts)

Cut yarn and fasten off, leaving a long tail for sewing.

Sew up side edges. Cut out (1) 4½ x 3-inch (11 x 8cm) rectangle of 1-inch (25mm)-thick cushion foam and place at bottom of cab. Stuff the rest of the cab with fiberfill.

## CAB ROOF

In black, loosely ch 6.

**Rnd 1:** Starting in 2nd ch and working in back ridge loops, sc 4, sc 4 in next ch. Rotate chain so front side of chain is facing up. Starting in front side of the next ch, sc 3, sc 3 in front side of next ch. (14 sts)

**Rnd 2:** Sc 3 in next st, sc 3, sc 3 in next st, sc 2, sc 3 in next st, sc 3, sc 3 in next st, sc 2. (22 sts)

**Rnd 3:** Sc 1, sc 3 in next st, sc 5, sc 3 in next st, sc 4, sc 3 in next st, sc 5, sc 3 in next st, sc 3. (30 sts)

**Rnd 4:** Sc 2, sc 3 in next st, sc 7, sc 3 in next st, sc 6, sc 3 in next st, sc 7, sc 3 in next st, sc 4. (38 sts)

**Rnd 5:** Sc 3, sc 3 in next st, sc 9, sc 3 in next st, sc 8, sc 3 in next st, sc 9, sc 3 in next st, sc 5. (46 sts)

**Rnd 6:** In bl; sc 46. (46 sts)

**Rnd 7:** In bl; sc 3, sc3tog, sc 9, sc3tog, sc 8, sc3tog, sc 9, sc3tog, sc 5. (38 sts)

**Rnd 8:** Sc 2, sc3tog, sc 7, sc3tog, sc 6, sc3tog, sc 7, sc3tog, sc 4. (30 sts)

**Rnd 9:** Sc 1, sc3tog, sc 5, sc3tog, sc 4, sc3tog, sc 5, sc3tog, sc 3. (22 sts)

# SKIDSTEER ////

Using foam stabilizer, cut (1) 3¼ x 3-inch (8 x 8cm) rectangle to stuff roof. Insert foam into roof.

**Rnd 10:** Sc3tog, sc 3, sc3tog, sc 2, sc3tog, sc 3, sc3tog, sc 2. (14 sts)

**Rnd 11:** Sc 14. (14 sts)

Cut yarn and fasten off, leaving a long tail for sewing. Sew the seam closed. With seam side down, sew bottom edge of roof to the open edge of the cab. Stuff more if needed before closing seam.

## REAR ENGINE

In yellow, loosely ch 23.

**Row 1:** Starting in 2nd ch from hook and working in back ridge loops, sc 22, turn. (22 sts)

**Rows 2–8:** Ch 1, sc 22, turn. (22 sts)

Cut yarn and fasten off, leaving a long tail for sewing.

**Row 9:** Count 7 sts in from end. Working in fl of 7th st, (sl st 1, ch 1, sc 1). Cont to work down the row in fl; sc 9, turn. (10 sts)

**Rows 10–14:** Ch 1, sc 10, turn. (10 sts)

**Row 15:** Ch 1, fl; sc 10, turn. (10 sts)

**Rows 16–22:** Ch 1, sc 10, turn. (10 sts)

**Row 23:** Ch 1, fl; sc 10, turn. (10 sts)

**Rows 24–27:** Ch 1, sc 10, turn. (10 sts)

Cut yarn and fasten off, leaving long tail for sewing. With surface loops of row 9, 15, and 23 facing out, sew row 27 to the middle of row 1. Wrap the sides of rows 1–8 around and sew the matching top and side edges together to form a box shape and stuff before closing seam. With rows 9 and 15 of rear engine lined up with rows 1 and 8 of the back cab wall, sew rear engine to the back cab wall.

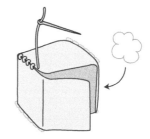

Double up black yarn on a tapestry needle and embroider a chain stitch around the front and side windows and the sides and top of the rear window. On side windows, use a single strand of black yarn and add a cage detail with a back stitch (refer to photos for reference).

## TIRE (MAKE 4)

Using black, make a 6-st adjustable ring.

**Rnd 1:** Sc 2 in each st around. (12 sts)

**Rnd 2:** *Sc 1, sc 2 in next st; rep from * 5 more times. (18 sts)

**Rnds 3–4:** Sc 18.

**Rnd 5:** *Sc 1, sc2tog; rep from * 5 more times. (12 sts)

Stuff tire.

**Rnd 6:** Sc2tog 6 times. (6 sts)

Fasten off yarn, leaving a long tail for sewing. Close the 6-st hole. Thread the yarn tail back and forth through the center of the tire 3 to 4 times, pulling tightly as you sew to shape the tire.

## TIRE HUBCAP (MAKE 4)

Using light gray, make a 4-st adjustable ring.

**Rnd 1:** Sc 2 in each st around. (8 sts)

Cut yarn and fasten off, leaving a long tail for sewing.

Sew the hubcaps to the sides of the tires.

Sew one pair of tires to front corners of cab and the second pair of tires to point where the back of cab and rear engine match up.

## LOADER BUCKET SIDE (MAKE 2)

With black, make a 4-st adjustable ring.

**Rnd 1:** Sc 3 in each st around (12 sts)

**Rnd 2:** *Sc 1, sc 3 in next st, sc 1; rep from * around. (20 sts)

**Rnd 3:** *Sc 2, sc 3 in next st, sc 2; rep from * around. (28 sts)

**Rnd 4:** *Sc 3, sc 3 in next st, sc 3; rep from * around. (36 sts)

Cut yarn and fasten off, leaving a long tail for sewing.

Using foam stabilizer, cut out (1) 2-inch (5cm) square. Cut square in half on the diagonal to form (2) triangles. Fold loader bucket side in half with WS tog to form a triangle, place foam inside, and sew seam shut. Rep on other piece.

# SKIDSTEER ////

## LOADER BUCKET CENTER

With black, loosely ch 16.

**Row 1:** Starting in 2nd ch from hook, sc 15, turn. (15 sts)

**Rows 2–7:** Ch 1, sc 15, turn. (15 sts)

**Row 8:** Ch 1, in fl; sc 15, turn. (15 sts)

**Rows 9–14:** Ch 1, sc 15, turn. (15 sts)

**Row 15:** Ch 1, in bl; sc 15, turn. (15 sts)

**Row 16:** Ch 1, in fl; sc 15, turn. (15 sts)

**Rows 17–21:** Ch 1, sc 15, turn. (15 sts)

**Row 22:** Ch 1, in bl; sc 15, turn. (15 sts)

**Rows 23–28:** Ch 1, sc 15, turn. (15 sts)

**Row 29:** Fold piece in half and line up row 1 and row 28 with the surface loops of rows 15–16 facing out. Holding edges together, sc 15 with row 1 and row 28 tog, turn. (15 sts)

**Row 30:** *Sl st 1, (sl st 1, ch 2, hdc 2, ch 2, sl st 1) in next st, sl st 1; rep from * to end.

Cut yarn and fasten off, leaving a long tail for sewing.

Using foam stabilizer, cut out (2) 2 x 3¾-inch (5 x 10cm) rectangles. Place the rectangle between the front and back layers of the loader bucket. With black yarn, sew up side seams with a whip stitch and sew a running stitch between the top and bottom layers through the bend at row 8 and row 22. The surface loops of row 8 will be in the back of the bucket.

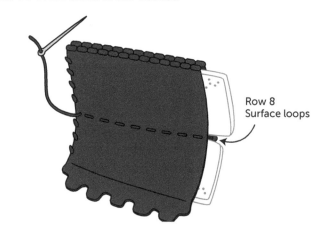

Row 8
Surface loops

Match up and pin the whip-stitched sides of the loader bucket center with the two shorter edges of the loader bucket sides. Sew the edges of the loader bucket center to the inside surfaces of the loader bucket sides.

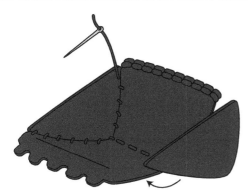

## LIFT ARM (MAKE 2)

In yellow, loosely ch 25, turn.

**Row 1:** Starting in 2nd ch from hook and working in back ridge loops, sc 18, sc 3 in next st, sc 5, turn. (26 sts)

**Row 2:** Ch 1, sl st 6, sc 3 in next st, sc 12, hdc 7, turn. (28 sts)

**Row 3:** Ch 1, sc 20, sc 3 in next st, sl st 7, turn. (30 sts)

**Row 4:** Ch 1, bl; sc 30, turn. (30 sts)

**Row 5:** Ch 1, fl; sc 20, sc3tog, sl st 7, turn. (28 sts)

**Row 6:** Ch 1, sl st 6, sc3tog, sc 12, hdc 7, turn. (26 sts)

**Row 7:** Ch 1, sc 18, sc3tog, sc 5, turn. (24 sts)

**Row 8:** Ch 1, bl; sc 24. (24 sts)

Cut yarn and fasten off, leaving a long tail for sewing.

Using foam stabilizer, cut (2) lift arm pieces from template (page 112). Fold lift arms the long way with rows 1 and 8 together and surface loops of rows 4 and 5 facing out. Place foam inside and sew edges together.

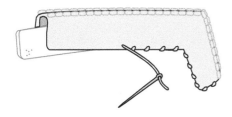

## AXLE PIN (MAKE 2)

In dark gray, make a 6-st adjustable ring.

**Rnd 1:** In bl; sc 6. (6 sts)

**Rnd 2:** Sc2tog 3 times. (3 sts)

Cut yarn and fasten off, leaving a long tail for sewing.

Cinch hole closed with yarn tail. Thread the yarn tail back and forth through the center of the axle pin 3 to 4 times, pulling tightly as you sew to flatten the axle pin.

Thread the tail of one axle pin through the large end of one lift arm and through the sides of the rear engine, making sure the front of the lift arm clears the front tire of the skidsteer. Thread yarn back through the sides of the rear engine and through the lift arm, securing the yarn under the axle pin and weaving in the end. Rep on other side with other axle pin and lift arm.

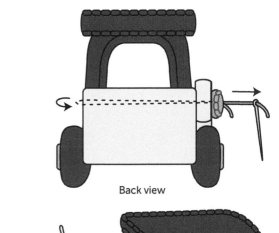

Back view

Sew ends of lift arms to the back of the completed bucket. Weave in any remaining yarn tails.

**TIP:** For vehicles intended for children 3 years and older, you can also use ½–¾-inch (13–19mm) shank buttons for axle pins.

# BUILDING MATERIALS

**YARN WEIGHT:** ⑤ BULKY

No building site is complete without some building materials to keep its mighty machines busy and happy! Make a ton of rocks to move around, some crates to stack, and safety cones to keep everything orderly.

## SAFETY CONE

**FINISHED SIZE:**
2 x 2 x 3 in. (5 x 5 x 8cm)

### MATERIALS & TOOLS

- Bulky-weight yarn in orange (100 yds/91m) and white (50 yds/46m)
- Hook size I (5.5mm)
- Scissors
- Polyester fiberfill

### INSTRUCTIONS

Starting with orange, make a 6-st adjustable ring.

**Rnd 1:** In bl; sc 6. (6 sts)

**Rnd 2:** *Sc 2, sc 2 in next st; rep from * around. (8 sts)

Change to white.

**Rnd 3:** Sc 8. (8 sts)

**Rnd 4:** *Sc 3, sc 2 in next st; rep from * around. (10 sts)

Change to orange.

**Rnd 5:** Sc 10. (10 sts)

**Rnd 6:** *Sc 4, sc 2 in next st; rep from * around. (12 sts)

**Rnds 7–8:** Sc 12. (12 sts)

**Rnd 9:** FPsc 12. (12 sts)

**Rnd 10:** *Sc 1, (sc 1, hdc 1, sc 1) in next st, sc 1; rep from * around. (20 sts)

**Rnd 11:** *Sc 2, (sc 1, hdc 1, sc 1) in next st, sc 2; rep from * around. (28 sts)

# BUILDING MATERIALS ////

Note: Stop here for an unstuffed safety cone.

**Rnd 12:** In bl; sl st 28. (28 sts)

**Rnd 13:** *In bl; sc 2, sc3tog, sc 2; rep from * around. (20 sts)

**Rnd 14:** *Sc 1, sc3tog, sc 1; rep from * around. (12 sts)

**Rnd 15:** Sc2tog 6 times. (6 sts)

Cut yarn and fasten off, leaving a long tail for sewing.

Stuff just the cone portion. Close hole at bottom of cone. Flatten base of cone and apply a running stitch around rnd 9 at the base of the cone and rnd 14 on the bottom of the cone to secure the shaping.

Weave in any remaining yarn tails.

## CRATES

**FINISHED SIZE:** 2½ x 2½ x 2½ in. (6 x 6 x 6cm)

### MATERIALS & TOOLS

- Bulky-weight yarn in brown (100 yds/91m) and tan (100 yds/91m)
- Hook size I (5.5mm)
- Scissors
- 1-in. (25mm)-thick cushion foam

### INSTRUCTIONS

With brown, make a 4-st adjustable ring.

**Rnd 1:** Sc 3 in each st around. (12 sts)

**Rnd 2:** *Sc 1, sc 3 in next st, sc 1; rep from * around. (20 sts)

**Rnd 3:** *Sc 2, sc 3 in next st, sc 2; rep from * around. (28 sts)

**Rnd 4:** In bl; sc 28. (28 sts)

**Rnds 5–10:** Sc 28. (28 sts)

**Rnd 11:** In bl; *sc 4, sc3tog; rep from * around. (20 sts)

**Rnd 12:** *Sc 2, sc3tog; rep from * around. (12 sts)

Using 1-inch (25mm)-thick cushion foam, cut out (3) 2-inch (5cm) squares and place inside crate.

**Rnd 13:** Sc3tog 4 times. (4 sts)

Cut yarn and fasten off, leaving a long tail for sewing.

Double up brown yarn and chain stitch a diagonal line on the sides of the crate. Working around the stitch posts directly under the surface loops from rnd 4, (sl st 1, ch 1, sc 1) around first stitch post, and then proceed to sc in the remaining 27 stitch posts around. (28 sts) Flip the crate over and rep this detail under the surface loops from rnd 11.

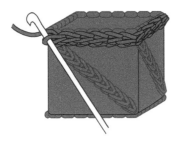

Weave in any remaining yarn tails.

## Rope detail

For optional rope detail, make (1) 9 to 9½-inch (23 to 24cm) cord out of light tan yarn (page 13). Wrap it snuggly around the box, secure to the bottom, and weave in the ends. Take a 2nd piece of light tan yarn and make a 14-inch (36cm) cord. Wrap it very loosely around the box, secure to bottom, and weave in ends. Pinch the loose part of the cord into a loop. Take light tan yarn and wrap it around the base of the loop, tie off, and weave the ends inside the wrap. To help keep the rope from sliding around, secure the rope to the sides of the box with light tan yarn if needed.

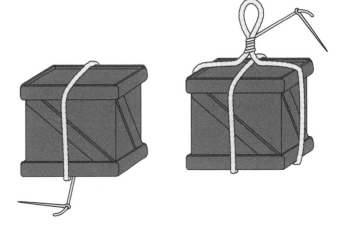

**TIP:** For directions on how to make a twisted cord, refer to page 13.

# BUILDING MATERIALS ////

## ROCKS

**FINISHED SIZE:** 2 x 1½ in. (5 x 4cm); 2½ x 2 in. (6 x 5cm); 4½ x 3 in. (11 x 8cm)

### MATERIALS & TOOLS

- Bulky-weight yarn in tan (100 yds/91m)
- Hook size I (5.5mm)
- Scissors
- Polyester fiberfill

### INSTRUCTIONS

**Large rock**
With tan, make an 8-st adjustable ring.

**Rnd 1:** Sc 2 in each st around. (16 sts)

**Rnd 2:** *Sc 1, sc 2 in next st; rep from * around. (24 sts)

**Rnd 3:** *Sc 2, sc 2 in next st; rep from * around. (32 sts)

**Rnd 4:** *Sc 3, sc 2 in next st; rep from * around. (40 sts)

**Rnds 5–12:** Sc 40.

**Rnd 13:** *Sc 3, sc2tog; rep from * around. (32 sts)

**Rnd 14:** *Sc 2, sc2tog; rep from * around. (24 sts)

**Rnd 15:** *Sc 1, sc2tog; rep from * around. (16 sts)

Stuff rock.

**Rnd 16:** Sc2tog 8 times. (8 sts)

Cut yarn and fasten off, leaving a long tail for sewing.

Draw yarn tail in and out of rock surface, pulling as you sew to give the rock a bumpy shape.

Weave in any remaining yarn tails.

### Medium rock
With tan, make a 6-st adjustable ring.

**Rnd 1:** Sc 2 in each st around. (12 sts)

**Rnd 2:** *Sc 1, sc 2 in next st; rep from * around. (18 sts)

**Rnd 3:** *Sc 2, sc 2 in next st; rep from * around. (24 sts)

**Rnd 4:** *Sc 3, sc 2 in next st; rep from * around. (30 sts)

**Rnds 5–8:** Sc 30. (30 sts)

**Rnd 9:** *Sc 3, sc2tog; rep from * around. (24 sts)

**Rnd 10:** *Sc 2, sc2tog; rep from * around. (18 sts)

**Rnd 11:** *Sc 1, sc2tog; rep from * around. (12 sts)

Stuff rock.

**Rnd 12:** Sc2tog 6 times. (6 sts)

Cut yarn and fasten off, leaving a long tail for sewing.

Draw yarn tail in and out of rock surface, pulling as you sew to give the rock a bumpy shape.

Weave in any remaining yarn tails.

### Small rock

With tan, make a 4-st adjustable ring.

**Rnd 1:** Sc 2 in each st around. (8 sts)

**Rnd 2:** *Sc 1, sc 2 in next st; rep from * around. (12 sts)

**Rnd 3:** *Sc 2, sc 2 in next st; rep from * around. (16 sts)

**Rnd 4:** *Sc 3, sc 2 in next st; rep from * around. (20 sts)

**Rnds 5–6:** Sc 20. (20 sts)

**Rnd 7:** *Sc 3, sc2tog; rep from * around. (16 sts)

**Rnd 8:** *Sc 2, sc2tog; rep from * around. (12 sts)

**Rnd 9:** *Sc 1, sc2tog; rep from * around. (8 sts)

Stuff rock.

**Rnd 10:** Sc2tog 4 times. (4 sts)

Cut yarn and fasten off, leaving a long tail for sewing.

Draw yarn tail in and out of rock surface, pulling as you sew to give the rock a bumpy shape.

Weave in any remaining yarn tails.

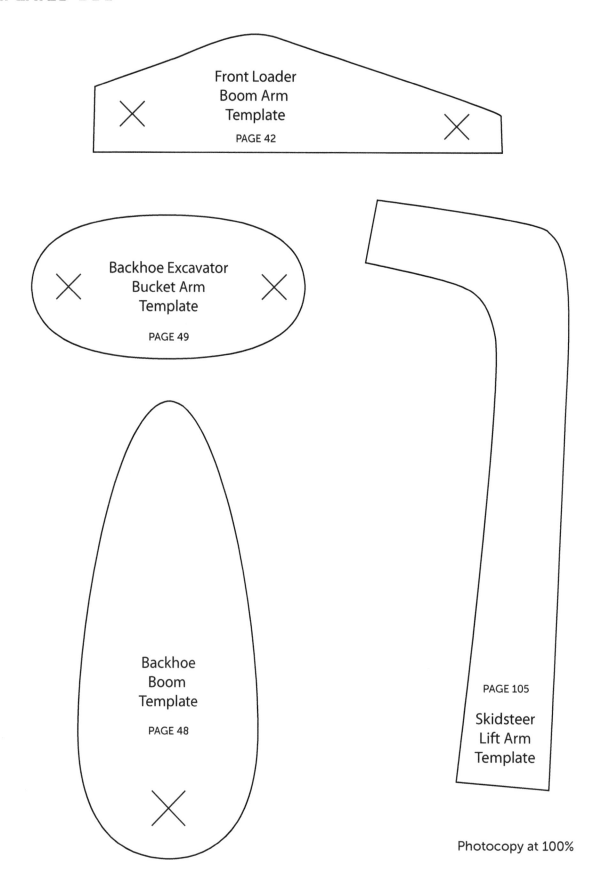

Front Loader
Boom Arm
Template

PAGE 42

Backhoe Excavator
Bucket Arm
Template

PAGE 49

Backhoe
Boom
Template

PAGE 48

PAGE 105

Skidsteer
Lift Arm
Template

Photocopy at 100%

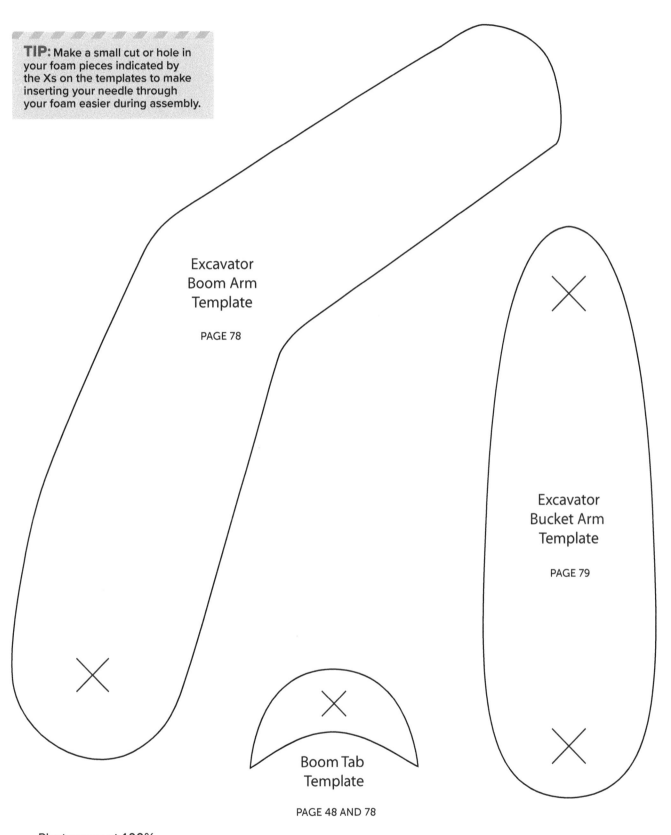

**TIP:** Make a small cut or hole in your foam pieces indicated by the Xs on the templates to make inserting your needle through your foam easier during assembly.

Excavator
Boom Arm
Template

PAGE 78

Excavator
Bucket Arm
Template

PAGE 79

Boom Tab
Template

PAGE 48 AND 78

Photocopy at 100%

# RESOURCES

## ABBREVIATIONS

*Repeat instructions following the asterisk(s) as directed

| | | | | |
|---|---|---|---|---|
| approx | approximately | | MC | main color |
| beg | begin(ning) | | mm | millimeter |
| bl | back loop(s) | | pm | place marker |
| BPsc | back post single crochet | | rep(s) | repeat(s) |
| CC | contrasting color | | rnd(s) | round(s) |
| ch(s) | chain(s) or chain stitch(es) | | RS | right side |
| ch- | refers to chain, or chain space previously made, such as "ch-1 space" | | sc | single crochet(s) |
| | | | sc2tog | single crochet 2 stitches together—1 stitch decreased |
| cont | continue(ing)(s) | | sk | skip |
| dc | double crochet(s) | | sl | slip |
| dec(s) | decrease(ing)(s) | | sl st(s) | slip stitch(es) |
| fl | front loop(s) | | sp(s) | space(s) |
| FPsc | front post single crochet | | st(s) | stitch(es) |
| hdc | half double crochet(s) | | tog | together |
| hdc2tog | half double crochet 2 stitches together— 1 stitch decreased | | tr | triple crochet |
| | | | WS | wrong side |
| | | | YO(s) | yarn over(s) |
| inc(s) | increase(ing)(s) | | yd(s) | yard(s) |
| lp(s) | loop(s) | | | |

## CROCHET HOOK SIZES

| Millimeter | U.S. Size* |
|---|---|
| 2.25mm | B-1 |
| 2.75mm | C-2 |
| 3.25mm | D-3 |
| 3.5mm | E-4 |
| 3.75mm | F-5 |
| 4mm | G-6 |
| 4.5mm | 7 |
| 5mm | H-8 |
| 5.5mm | I-9 |
| 6mm | J-10 |
| 6.5mm | K-10½ |
| 8mm | L-11 |
| 9mm | M/N-13 |

*Letter or number may vary. Rely on the millimeter sizing.

## YARN WEIGHT CHART

| Yarn Weight Symbol & Category Names | 0 LACE | 1 SUPER FINE | 2 FINE | 3 LIGHT | 4 MEDIUM | 5 BULKY | 6 SUPER BULKY | 7 JUMBO |
|---|---|---|---|---|---|---|---|---|
| Types of Yarns in Category | Fingering, 10 count crochet thread | Sock, Fingering, Baby | Sport, Baby | DK, Light Worsted | Worsted, Afghan, Aran | Chunky, Craft, Rug | Bulky, Roving | Jumbo, Roving |

Source: Craft Yarn Council's www.YarnStandards.com

## PROJECT COLORS

The projects in this book were made using Berroco Comfort Chunky (50% nylon, 50% acrylic), 3.5 oz (100g) / 150 yds (137m) per ball, in the colors outlined below. Feel free to use your favorite brand of appropriate weight yarn (available online and through your local yarn shop).

**Flatbed Truck**
5717 Rasberry Coulis, 5770 Ash Grey, 5713 Dusk, 5700 Chalk, 5734 Liquorice

**Dump Truck**
5752 Adirondack, 5770 Ash Grey, 5700 Chalk, 5734 Liquorice

**Cement Mixer**
5756 Copen Blue, 5743 Goldenrod, 5770 Ash Grey, 5700 Chalk, 5734 Liquorice

**Front Loader**
5743 Goldenrod, 5770 Ash Grey, 5713 Dusk, 5700 Chalk, 5734 Liquorice

**Backhoe**
5743 Goldenrod, 5770 Ash Grey, 5713 Dusk, 5700 Chalk, 5734 Liquorice

**Steamroller**
5743 Goldenrod, 5770 Ash Grey, 5750 Primary Red, 5713 Dusk, 5700 Chalk, 5734 Liquorice

**Crane**
5750 Primary Red, 5770 Ash Grey, 5713 Dusk, 5700 Chalk, 5734 Liquorice

**Excavator**
5743 Goldenrod, 5770 Ash Grey, 5713 Dusk, 5700 Chalk, 5734 Liquorice

**Bulldozer**
5743 Goldenrod, 5770 Ash Grey, 5713 Dusk, 5700 Chalk, 5734 Liquorice

**Forklift**
5724 Pumpkin, 5770 Ash Grey, 5713 Dusk, 5700 Chalk, 5734 Liquorice, 5756 Copen Blue

**Skidsteer**
5743 Goldenrod, 5770 Ash Grey, 5713 Dusk, 5700 Chalk, 5734 Liquorice

**Safety Cones**
5724 Pumpkin, 5700 Chalk

**Crates**
5727 Spanish Brown, 5720 Hummus

**Rocks**
5720 Hummus

# DEDICATION

To the staff at the Child Educational Center
in La Cañada Flintridge, California.

You sent my children home covered in sand,
mud, and dirt every day.

Thank you for making them so happy.

# ACKNOWLEDGMENTS

Thank you to the amazing staff at Cedar Lane Press
for helping me put together another beautiful book!
It's always a pleasure to work with you!

Thank you to Berroco for being so generous
with material donations for this book.

And, finally, a big thank you to my husband, Michael,
for all his support and to my children, James and Emily,
for thoroughly testing out all my toy patterns for
imaginative potential and material durability.

## MATERIAL SOURCES

If you're interested in using some of the yarns or tools used in this book, please check out the following resources that are available online and from your local craft store.

### Berroco
www.berroco.com

Comfort Chunky yarn

### Bosal Foam & Fiber
www.bosalfoam.com

Bosal In-R-Form sew-in foam stabilizer (in white)

### ByAnnie's
www.byannie.com

Soft and Stable polyester stabilizer (in black)

### Clover
www.clover-usa.com

Hooks and notions

### Fiskars
www.fiskars.com

Scissors and cutting mats

### Hobbs Bonded Fibers
www.hobbsbondedfibers.com

Poly-down fiberfill toy stuffing and black batting

### NuFoam
www.fairfieldworld.com

1-inch (25mm)-thick cushion foam made of densified polyester batting

## ABOUT THE AUTHOR

Megan Kreiner grew up on Long Island, New York in a household where art and art projects were a daily part of life. Coming from a long line of knitters and crocheters, Megan learned the craft at an early age from her grandmother, her aunt, and her mother. As of 2012, her MK Crochet pattern line has been published and featured in numerous books and various crochet and knitting magazines.

A graduate with a fine arts degree in computer graphics and animation from the University of Massachusetts, Amherst, Megan is pursuing a career in the feature animation industry in Los Angeles and currently works as an animator at DreamWorks Animation.

# INDEX

*Italicized text indicates a project

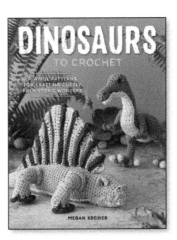

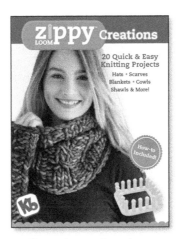

# MORE GREAT BOOKS *from*
# CEDAR LANE PRESS

**Knitted Baskets**
$22.95 | 128 Pages

**Crochet Baskets**
$22.95 | 128 Pages

**Fabulous Fat Quarter Aprons**
$12.99 | 56 Pages

**The Handmade Mama**
$27.95 | 200 Pages

**The Natural Beauty Solution**
$19.95 | 128 Pages

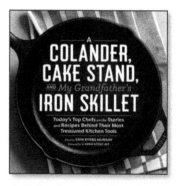

**A Colander, Cake Stand, and
My Grandfather's Iron
Skillet**
$24.95 | 184 Pages

CEDAR LANE PRESS

Look for these titles wherever books are sold or visit www.cedarlanepress.com.

Printed in the USA
CPSIA information can be obtained
at www.ICGtesting.com
JSHW041908240624
65307JS00011B/37